KINDRA HALL

advanced training

Phoenix

©2013 Telzall

All rights reserved. No portion of this book maybe reproduced or transmitted in any form or by any means electronic or mechanical, including photocopying, recording or by any storage retrieval systems except for brief quotations in reviews or articles, without the prior written permission of the author.

In some instances, names, locations, and other details have been purposefully changed to protect the identities and privacy of those discussed in this book.

Cover design and layout by Sarah Sandhaus of Electric Dreams Design.
Printed in the United States of America

ISBN 9-780988-998711

In this Workbook

4 GETTING STARTED
  6 Preface
  8 Introduction
 11 How to Use this Book
 12 Acknowledgements

14 Part One: YOUR STORY
 16 *Chapter One:* You Have a Story to Tell
 19 *Chapter Two:* Why Tell Your Story

22 Part Two: GO FIND IT
 24 *Chapter Three:* Common Experiences
 52 *Chapter Four:* Turning Points
 92 *Chapter Five:* Creating Lists
154 *Chapter Six:* Triggers

184 Part Three: UGLY STORIES

212 Part Four: TOPIC SPECIFIC STORIES

244 Part Five: STORIES THAT ARE HAPPENING NOW

260 Part Six: ADDITIONAL THINGS
265 Conclusion

Stories are the most powerful delivery tool for information. — NANCY DUARTE

Getting Started

GETTING STARTED
PREFACE

PREFACE

I was sitting in the neighborhood coffee shop, MacBook Pro on the table, earphones in place, trying to get some work done... but I knew better. If I *really* wanted to get work done I would have gone to a library, or at least to a *different* neighborhood's coffee shop. Instead, I chatted with the dozen different people I knew from a dozen different places, accomplishing nothing.

Just about the time I started to feel guilty for paying someone to watch my kids while I socialized, an acquaintance walked in – a commercial real estate developer I met through the spin studio where I work out. We shared friendly conversation, discussed which spin classes we had (or in *his* case, hadn't) attended that week, and when he asked what I was working on I mentioned storytelling. He knew this was something I was involved with and he had, in fact, read some of my work.

"Actually," he said. "I just bought a book at the airport about storytelling. I think I need to become a better storyteller."

What happened next was a little inappropriate.
I wouldn't say I *yelled*, but I would definitely say I spoke loudly. I knew the book he had purchased, I had (obviously) read it, and I knew it would get him nowhere. I passionately expressed the shortcomings of said storytelling book and, frankly, *every* storytelling book.

Here is the story with books about stories:
They'll tell you storytelling is important.
They'll tell you *you* need to use it.
They'll tell you *they* use it.
They'll tell you about plot and character development.
They'll tell you about playwrights and movie scripts.
They'll even give you performance advice.
But they won't tell you where to start.

You'll read the whole book, you'll nod your head and agree, and then you'll turn the last page and still be left wondering where to even begin.

How do you *find* your stories?
Do you even *have* stories to tell?

I am no stranger to these questions (which you'll read about later).
I discovered storytelling in 1992.
I was eleven.
Since that time, my work with stories has varied from fairytales, to telling personal stories, to helping others tell theirs. I have told stories to audiences as large as 15,000 and defended the use of storytelling in business

PREFACE

for my master's thesis. I was the youngest person to ever serve on the Board of Directors of the National Storytelling Network and have had the distinct honor of telling on the stage at the most recognized storytelling event in the country – the National Storytelling Festival in Jonesborough, Tennessee. I work with professional speakers, business leaders, political figures, salesmen, pro-athletes, and others to utilize the power of personal story.

And now, I work with *you*.

My acquaintance left the coffee shop that afternoon and I felt an overwhelming sense of urgency; I needed to write *this* storytelling book before he went and wasted his money on another one. The very next day I drove to a different neighborhood's coffee shop and got to work.

I promise that when you turn the last page of *this* book you will not be asking *how* to start.
I also promise not to yell at you if I run into you at a coffee shop.

GETTING STARTED

INTRODUCTION

INTRODUCTION

There is *one thing* that separates the good from the best when it comes to effective communication: story. In sales, in politics, in corporate branding, whoever tells the best story, wins – which means, if you're not telling your story, you're losing.

I was a junior in high school and attending a one-day leadership seminar. Students from all over the state came together to share what was working in their schools, brainstorm new ideas, and learn leadership skills to "last a lifetime."

Right. I'd been to leadership seminars before.

All I really wanted was to meet cute boys.

There were always cute boys at leadership seminars.

The day started with a morning of breakout sessions, lunch at noon, and then we all gathered in the auditorium for a keynote speaker who was, no doubt, going to teach us leadership skills to "last a lifetime."

I remember sitting toward the back of the theater on the right hand side of the room with a boy named Justin whom I had met the summer before at a different leadership seminar/camp. He was wearing a black leather jacket and was cuter than I remembered. I was entirely distracted as the speaker took the stage. There was little hope of me retaining any leadership strategies, much less skills that would last a lifetime.

And then the presenter began to speak. Actually, he began to tell. Stories. Stories about goal setting, about conquering fear, and about leadership.

He told one story about speaking in a high school gymnasium. He told us about when he was sitting on the temporary metal-framed stage before the program began and watching as hundreds of students filed into the room....

Hundreds of students.

Through one door.

Though there were multiple entrances to the gym; for some reason, every single student was trying to squeeze through a single set of heavy metal double doors. Isn't that always how it goes? There were two thousand students scheduled to attend his presentation... this was going to take a while. Just as he began to wonder if he would miss his flight home, the speaker saw a second set of doors begin to open. Slowly. Timidly. From behind them emerged a single student – an ordinary boy, who propped the door open just as a deluge of students began to flow in behind him. He then went down the row of doors, opening every one, watching as his classmates poured in and the gymnasium filled at record speed. Moments later the boy disappeared in the crowd and the speaker took the stage, touched by what he just witnessed.

GETTING STARTED
INTRODUCTION

The speaker paused. He looked to us, his current audience of leadership seminar-goers, every one of us sitting silently, hanging on his every word. He asked us if we had ever witnessed that situation. We all nodded, of course we had. He asked if any of us had ever stepped out of the herd, opened another door, and offered another path for our classmates to follow. We didn't move.

"That's what leadership is. That's what leaders do."

I left the leadership seminar that day with some new friends, some cool ideas for homecoming, but most of all... with a story that had not only found its way into my head, but into my heart as well. From that moment on, I looked for opportunities to open new doors, to offer another path, to be a leader.

Skills to last a lifetime.

How did he do it? How did the speaker not only *reach* a distracted, one-track-minded high school girl sitting next to a boy in a leather jacket, but how was he able to *inspire change* in my behavior? How was he able to stand on a stage and deliver a message that would still influence me nearly twenty years later?

After all, isn't that what we all want? Whether they are a roomful of students, a potential new customer, a congregation, a donor to a cause, shareholders at an annual meeting, or a convention center filled with salespeople, we want to not only *reach* our audiences, but to *resonate* with them. To *influence* them – we want them to connect, to change, to buy, to donate, to get on board, or simply to come to their feet in applause when our time on stage is done.

So how? How did he do it? How do we make that happen?

You already know the answer; you're reading this book.

Story.

> MAYBE STORIES ARE JUST DATA WITH SOUL.
> – BRENÉ BROWN

I'll admit, this in and of itself is not new information; you have probably heard it before. Over the course of the last decade, and especially with the recent rapid rise of social media and digital outlets, it seems the word "storytelling" is on the tip of everyone's tongue. Like a song that gets way overplayed on the radio, you'll hear it again and again – storytelling. Experts in all fields will tell you that storytelling is important: in business, in sales, in education, you name it, you need it – storytelling. And I agree with them, couldn't agree more. But after hearing it so many times without any additional information, it's easy to change the station and file storytelling away as a song you used to like.

I am not here just to tell you that storytelling is important, though we will cover that. I am not just going to tell

INTRODUCTION

you that you need to *find* and *tell* your personal stories if you want to resonate with your audience, though we'll cover that too. Instead, I'm going to take you where no one has taken you before... to the beginning.

Everyone (yes, even you) has an unlimited amount of awesome story material locked up in memories. You just need focused strategies for accessing it.

You have come to the right place.

What I will teach you in the following pages is how to uncover your stories so you can start using them to your advantage.

Everyone has stories to tell.

Let me be the first to help you find them.

GETTING STARTED
HOW TO USE THIS BOOK

HOW TO USE THIS BOOK
If you are:

    A Salesperson – with clients to close.
    A Speaker – with an audience to motivate.
    An Expert – with a message to share.
    A CEO – with shareholders to impress.
    A Preacher – with a congregation to move.
    A Teacher – with students to impact.
    A Cause – with a need to raise funds and make a difference.
    A Scientist – with research to explain.
    Anyone with a desire to share their story....

Then this book is for you.

Throughout this book I will use the terms *presenter*, or *speaker*, or several others – know that all of them apply to YOU and however you define yourself and the role in which you want to improve your storytelling skill. This training will walk you through – step by step – the many different ways you can search, identify, and discover your personal stories. We will cover Finding Your Story by using recollections of common experiences, turning points, detailed lists, and triggers. We'll discuss finding and working with the "ugly stories" – stories that you might have tried to forget. You'll learn how to find topic/theme-specific stories for an upcoming presentation you may be scheduled to give, and finally you will develop the skills needed to recognize stories as they are happening today.

You will be asked to complete exercises... DO THEM. This book will not work if *you* do not work. Be open-minded, thorough, and diligent. I can promise that if you follow the instructions this book provides, you will have more stories to choose from than you ever thought possible and stories will continue to appear long after the exercises are complete.

A few other things before we begin:

As you know, there is a DVD training that follows this book, chapter by chapter, with further explanation, expansion, and examples of the exercises outlined on these pages. I recommend watching the corresponding DVD section as you begin each new chapter of the book. Keep the DVD training handy while you work through this project so you can quickly and easily access the info that was better *said* than *written*.

My hope is that, by the time you reach the end of this training, the cover of this book will be worn, the corners frayed, and the pages filled with bits and pieces of your wonderful life that might otherwise have been forgotten.

Use this book when it's time to really WOW your audience..
Your stories will be here waiting for you.

ACKNOWLEDGEMENTS

Finally, there are a few people I want to thank.

Storyteller Donald Davis is the most exceptional teller I have ever known. I am grateful for his support, for all that he has taught me about storytelling, and especially for his (and his wife, Merle's) love and friendship. I need to thank my parents, Mike and Gayle, for encouraging the storyteller in me… especially during those years when I wouldn't. A special thanks to Darren Hardy, who helped me turn the "art" of storytelling into a business – for that I can never thank you enough. Finally, thank you to my husband, Michael, for helping me get what was in my head onto paper.

GETTING STARTED
ACKNOWLEDGEMENTS

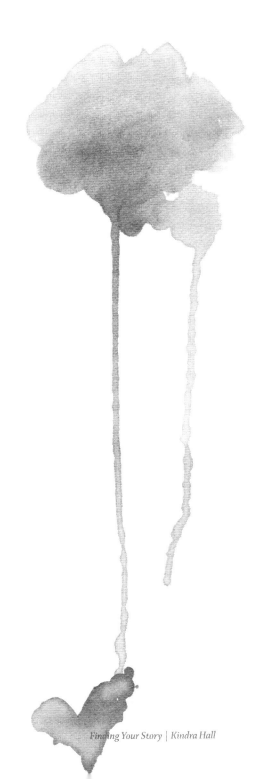

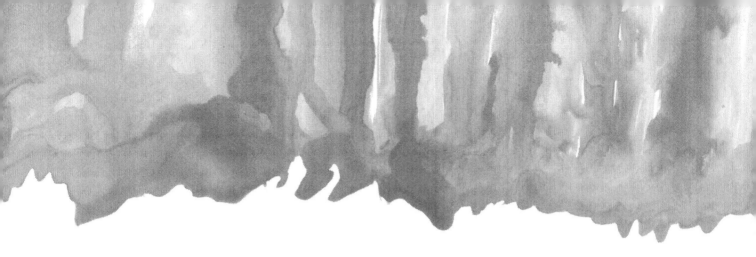

> *There is no greater agony than bearing an untold story inside you.*
> — MAYA ANGELOU

Part One
YOUR STORY

Chapter One
YOU HAVE A STORY TO TELL

There are many things that make a good speaker; an expert in a field with valuable information, a thought leader or innovator, an author, an educator, an employer. All of these things, even experience *alone*, can make a *good* speaker....but the best, most memorable, most highly praised speakers are also great *storytellers*.

These speakers connect with their audiences by sharing personal stories – tales of struggle or victory. They educate their audiences as they weave together stats, strategies, and story. They motivate and empower, elicit emotion, and open pathways to learning, all through sharing stories. Most important, when the event is over, when the meeting is complete and the audience returns to their lives, the stories stay with them – the *speaker* stays with them.

Speakers who are storytellers are hired again and again – because audience satisfaction is guaranteed.

> PEOPLE DON'T JUST WEAR OUR SHOES, THEY TELL OUR STORY.
> – BLAKE MYCOSKIE
> FOUNDER, CEO
> TOMS

So why don't more people use personal stories in their presentations? Why do so many rely on PowerPoints and endless pages of bullet points to get their point across? The answer is simple: Most people don't believe they have a story to *tell*.

At least not a story anyone would care to hear.

I know this because I have been there – desperate to resonate with my audience, but essentially, story-less.

Growing up on the speech team (one level less-cool than glee club), I spent most of my time immersed in oratory. It was pretty obvious, even to a high school kid that the best speeches were those rich in personal stories. I would listen as others told the lost tales of their ancestors; stories of struggle and pain from African American speakers, the wisdom of Native American lore. Other speakers told of growing up surrounded by the dangers of the inner city – stories of violence or fear, still others told stories of overcoming overwhelming odds. Every story brought me to a new place, a place I had never been before, a place filled with drama or mystery,

PART ONE
YOU HAVE A STORY TO TELL

humor or sadness.

As much as I wanted to tell *my* stories, I knew I couldn't.
My stories weren't that good.

My heritage was bland – some unclear mixture of Irish, Norwegian, and English. No story there. I didn't grow up with prejudice; I grew up in Minnesota. I faced very little struggle; my parents were educated, employed, and loving. I had a brother, a sister, a cat, and a pretty normal middle-class life. None of my stories could take people to a place they had never been – *everyone* had been to my stories.

And while I was certainly disappointed that I would never impact an audience in the way I wished I could, even more disheartening, I felt… insignificant. Here I was living this life, and the only person who would want to hear stories about it was my mom and the diary that I hid from her.

Then one evening at a casual open-mic event, after a glass and a half of wine (because that's all it takes to lower my inhibitions), I stood in front of the microphone and twenty or so patrons and took a chance. I told the story of my secret fifth grade crush – a crush that went terribly wrong during the school play in front of an auditorium filled with classmates and parents. Though it wasn't designed to elicit any reaction except for enjoyment, the audience response was completely unexpected. After the show many listeners came up to reminisce on their *own* fifth-grade-loves-gone-wrong. I overheard them sitting at their tables saying names of classmates that had long since been forgotten.

I wondered if I was onto something….

In the coming weeks and months, I kept telling. I told a story about moving in with my (now) husband and what I learned about myself during that 'interesting' process. I told a story about running the 75-yard dash in second grade – confident I would win because I could always catch my father when I chased him and the unexpected lesson that came with coming in last. I told the simple stories, and as I did, audiences responded. They laughed when it was funny and quietly nodded along when a moment of *mine* sounded a lot like a moment of their own. I was greeted after each performance with people eager to share a bit of a memory that had come to them, like a rediscovered treasure, as they listened.

It took some time for me to believe it, for me to understand it, but eventually there was no denying it: my normal, bland, everyday-life was full of stories! Stories I thought were too "normal" to share were the *exact* stories people wanted to hear.

As I began working with others, it became clear that I was not the only one who questioned whether or not I had a story. My clients entered our first session nervously and offered a string of disclaimers that all expressed the same fear – that they didn't have a story to tell.

PART ONE
YOU HAVE A STORY TO TELL

I was working with an organization on a project to raise awareness for autism. My role was to interview mothers of children with autism and share their stories. I remember sitting on the phone with one mother as we walked through "Finding Your Story" exercises and she recounted her experience. Throughout the process the young mother kept pausing and apologizing for rambling as she shared small fragments of memories and pieces of her everyday life, sorry that there really wasn't a story there. Though she never said these words, I knew they were lurking behind every hesitation....

"My stories aren't stories that people actually care about."
Essentially, she feared that her "normal" life didn't carry value for others.

And it makes sense – our ups and downs, our moments of frustration, the moments of joy in our lives – these aren't stories for us, they are just life. What this young mother didn't realize was, and what many people underestimate is, the value that exists in the everyday stories.

For those whose life doesn't look like yours, they'll enjoy a glimpse of a world they haven't seen before. For those whose life does look like yours, even in the smallest way, they experience immense satisfaction in hearing themselves in your stories. You make them feel normal, connected, validated. And, in the case of the young woman I was working with – and for other mothers who are raising children with autism – moments of feeling normal or validated are priceless.

Everyone has stories to tell.
It's just a matter of finding them.

Chapter Two
WHY TELL YOUR STORY

CONNECT WITH YOUR AUDIENCE

The speakers you remember are the ones who make you forget – forget that the chair you're sitting on is uncomfortable, or that you have to swing by the dry cleaners and grocery store on the way home. The best speakers are the ones who don't just *speak* to their audiences, they *connect* with them – when the speaking is done, the message stays with them.

Whether your audience is a potential client, a classroom of students, or your family sitting around the dinner table, *connecting* with them happens when what you're saying makes them *feel* something. Bullet points don't do that. When was the last time you *felt* a bullet point? Facts aren't enough. When was the last time you were motivated to buy/change/improve by a fact? Personal story makes you *feel*.

Don't get me wrong; research, data, facts – they all have a place and serve an important purpose. However, while people *learn* from facts and can appreciate logic, people *connect* through shared experiences and beliefs. Well-crafted, intentional storytelling blurs the lines between the speaker's experience and the listener's *own* story. This allows unique access beyond the barriers all audiences build and an opportunity to connect on an emotional level.

> *A few years ago I was asked to speak to a small group of sales representatives. This team was responsible for selling commercial airtime for the local affiliate of Univision, one of the largest Hispanic television networks in the nation. Our general topic was "storytelling in business" but their more focused objective was clearly "storytelling to increase revenue."*
>
> *As we sat around the boardroom table, I casually asked them to tell me about their most successful customer experience: Who bought ad time and as a result their business thrived?*
>
> *One male rep spoke up; he talked about an older woman who ran a very small furniture company out of*

PART ONE
WHY TELL YOUR STORY

the back room of another business in a low-income Phoenix neighborhood. He recalled their conversation about her dreams for the business, her options for advertising, her initial hesitation, and how her face lit up when he mentioned she could be on TV. He told us how excited she was when her commercial aired and that she saw immediate return. Because of her advertisement, the woman's furniture business moved from a back room to its own building and eventually expanded to five stores across the valley. The other agents nodded their heads as he spoke – they had heard this story before and they were thrilled for her success.

When the story was complete, I shifted focus. I asked the sales team what a typical presentation looked like: What do they say or show their potential clients when pitching the sale? I was immediately inundated with pie charts, graphs, and statistics. As they told me about each glossy page, I asked them: Where was the furniture lady in those graphs? They were silent. I asked, at what point during the presentation did they tell the potential client how her face lit up and how excited she was as each new store opened? They were silent. Fortunately, in that silence, I could hear the light bulbs turning on.

We spent the rest of the meeting brainstorming all of their "favorite client stories" and discussing how they could effectively communicate these stories to connect with their clients. As colorful and as beautiful as pie charts or PowerPoints can be, no amount of graphs or data can ever replace the story of a satisfied customer.

The difference between a good presentation and a great one is the strength of the connection to the audience – the best (arguably, the *only*) way to establish that connection is through the effective use of storytelling.

AN OPPORTUNITY FOR AUTHENTICITY

One of the reasons personal story is so effective in connecting the speaker with the audience is because it provides an opportunity for authenticity.

We are a skeptical people. Whether it's a candidate for the presidency, a new hire, or a first date, we scan Instagram, scour Facebook, Google till our eyes cross, trying to determine if "they are who they say they are." This societal need for transparency and authenticity is most effectively satisfied by personal story. A presenter's willingness to share an authentic glimpse of their real selves through story (funny or serious, long or short) builds trust and likeability, and subsequently, effectiveness of the message. We will discuss this phenomenon further in Part Three, but I trust you understand where I'm going with this.

YOUR STORY AS A GIFT

It was a Saturday night in late February and I was in Austin, Minnesota. I was eighteen and was asked to

PART ONE
WHY TELL YOUR STORY

tell a story as part of a two-hour storytelling concert. It was one of the first performances on the stage of a beautifully restored old theater and tickets had been sold out for weeks. Though it was obviously a pretty unique opportunity, at the time, there were other things I wanted to be doing– a high school basketball game, a postgame party with my friends.... Instead, I was two and a half hours away, on wintery roads, in a small town to tell one 6-minute story. As far as I was concerned: Not. Worth it.

I remember the emcee calling my name and me walking up on the stage. I remember telling the story as I always had. I remember looking into the crowd and seeing a blur of faces I didn't recognize and would likely never see again. I remember thanking them as I finished, walking off the stage, watching the rest of the concert, and then making the long trip home. All in all, I enjoyed my time, but really, was sharing the story worth the effort?

A month later I had my answer.

On a Tuesday afternoon I received a card in the mail from a woman I didn't know – one of the nameless faces in the audience that night in Austin. In cursive that was obviously penned with an aged hand the woman explained how she got my mailing and that she wanted to thank me for my story... because several months earlier she had lost her husband, her companion of 57 years... that night, my story made her "belly laugh for the first time since his passing."

She thanked me for helping her find her laughter again.

Very simply put, your story can be a *gift*.
They can learn from your mistakes.
They can see things from a fresh perspective.
They can remember stories of their own.
They can rest assured that if you survived, they can too.
They can simply laugh.

It is impossible to know all of the ways our stories stick with people – but one thing is certain... they *do*. We will talk more about this concept later in the book, but for now, remember: for someone who needs to hear the exact story you're telling at the moment you're telling it, your story is a gift.

> **WHERE THERE IS PERFECTION THERE IS NO STORY TO TELL.**
> – BEN OKRI

So now you know: your stories are there, your stories are important, and we've identified just a few of the reasons why you have to go find them. The rest of this book will offer you the most effective strategies for doing so – strategies that I have used over the course of my twenty-year storytelling career. Strategies that I have taught to others. Strategies that will make you the best storyteller you know.

> *Story is your path to creating faith.*
> — ANNETTE SIMMONS

Part Two
GO FIND IT

Chapter Three
COMMON EXPERIENCES

> WE CANNOT THINK WITHOUT LANGUAGE, WE CANNOT PROCESS EXPERIENCE WITHOUT STORY.
> – CHRISTINA BALDWIN

The only way you are going to have stories to tell is if you go looking for them. This first exercise is designed to ease you into this "searching" process. Below are a series of events that many have experienced – firsts, favorites, least favorites. Under each situation is a series of questions – answer them to the best of your recollection and then push yourself to recollect a little more.

These questions aren't meant to limit you; they are meant to open you up. So if something comes to you while you're writing one memory, take a moment to entertain the tangent. In my experience working with my clients, I have found the tangents to be where the best stuff is. At the same time, if one of the questions is stumping you or simply isn't applicable, move on. That being said, there is a difference between not being *applicable* and not being *relevant*. DO NOT worry about, or even begin to consider, what is and is not relevant. If there is an answer to the question, no matter what it is, write it down.

YOUR FIRST CAR

What was your first car:

Make: ....

Model: ....

Year: ....

Color: ....

Did it have a nickname? What was it? ....

How did it get that nickname? ....

Was it yours or did you share it (with a sibling, with your parents, etc.)?

....

....

PART TWO
COMMON EXPERIENCES

How old were you when you got your first car? ....

What were the circumstances?
    Was it your dream car? ....
    Was it a gift? ....
    Was it a beater? ....

Who was the first person who received a ride in your car?

....
....
....
....

Who was in your car the most often? Why?
    Where did you drive the most?
    Who was there?
    What would you do?

....
....
....
....
....
....
....
....
....
....

Did anything ever go wrong with your first car?

....
....
....
....
....

PART TWO
COMMON EXPERIENCES

Did anything ever go wrong IN your first car?

....
....
....
....

What happened to that first car?

....
....
....
....
....

Now set a timer for 7 minutes & write down anything else you can remember about that first car or related to it:

....
....
....
....
....
....
....
....
....
....
....
....
....
....
....
....
....

PART TWO
COMMON EXPERIENCES

PART TWO
COMMON EXPERIENCES

PART TWO
COMMON EXPERIENCES

PART TWO
COMMON EXPERIENCES

YOUR FIRST JOB
What was your first job? ....
How old were you? ....
Why did you want/need/get a job? ....
How did you get that job? ....
When did you start? ....
What did you do with the money you earned from that job?

....
....
....

Who was your boss? ....
     Did you like him/her? ....
What was your favorite part of the job? ....
What were your responsibilities?

....
....
....

Now set a timer for 7 minutes & write down anything else you can remember about that first job or related to it:

....
....
....
....
....
....
....
....
....
....
....
....
....

PART TWO

COMMON EXPERIENCES

PART TWO
COMMON EXPERIENCES

PART TWO

COMMON EXPERIENCES

PART TWO
COMMON EXPERIENCES

Let's try a tangent...

When I was completing this exercise, it came to my attention that my first "job" was *not* actually the first way I *earned money*. I remembered that my father gave me a dime every day I brushed and flossed my teeth both morning and night. That memory would not have come to me had I not been completing the Your First Job exercise.

So, since we're here, if your first job *wasn't* the first way you earned money:
What was the first way you ever earned (or tried to earn) money?

How old were you?

What inspired you to start working?

What else do you remember about that experience?

PART TWO
COMMON EXPERIENCES

YOUR FIRST KISS

When was your first kiss? ....
Who was it with? ....
    How did you know him/her? ....
    Had you been hoping to kiss him/her? ....
Where did it happen? ....
What were the circumstances?

....
....
....
....
....
....
....
....
....
....

Did you initiate it? ....
Were you happy it happened? ....

What happened after that first kiss:
    Immediately after?
    The next day?
    The next week?

PART TWO
COMMON EXPERIENCES

Now set a timer for 7 minutes & write down anything else you can recall about that first kiss or related to it:

PART TWO
COMMON EXPERIENCES

PART TWO
COMMON EXPERIENCES

YOUR FAVORITE TEACHER

Who was your favorite teacher? ....

What grade? ....

What subject? ....

Why did you like him/her so much?

....
....
....
....

What do you remember most about what he/she looked like?

....
....
....
....

Do you remember anything school-related he/she taught you?

....
....
....
....

Do you remember anything non-school-related he/she taught you?

....
....
....
....

Did that teacher ever give you praise? What was it?

....
....
....
....

PART TWO
COMMON EXPERIENCES

If that teacher were to see you now, what would he/she say?

    Would he/she be proud?

    Surprised?

....

....

....

....

When was the last time you saw that teacher? What were the circumstances?

....

....

....

....

....

Now set a timer for 7 minutes and write down anything else you can remember about your favorite teacher or related to him/her:

....

....

....

....

....

....

....

....

....

....

....

....

....

....

....

PART TWO
COMMON EXPERIENCES

PART TWO
COMMON EXPERIENCES

PART TWO
COMMON EXPERIENCES

YOUR LEAST FAVORITE BOSS

Who was your least favorite boss? ....

Where did you work? ....

How old were you? ....

How old was your boss? ....

What did your boss look like?

....
....
....
....

Why did you dislike your boss?

....
....
....
....
....
....
....
....
....
....

Did your boss dislike you? Why yes or why no?

....
....
....
....
....
....
....
....

PART TWO
COMMON EXPERIENCES

What was one time your boss made you angry/upset/scared?
    What happened?

....
....
....
....

    What was the outcome?

....
....
....
....

Did you learn anything from your least favorite boss?

....
....
....
....
....
....

What eventually happened?
    Did you quit? Did you get fired? Are you still working for your least favorite boss?

....
....
....
....
....
....
....

PART TWO
COMMON EXPERIENCES

Now set a timer for 7 minutes & write down anything else you can remember about your least favorite boss or related to him/her:

PART TWO
COMMON EXPERIENCES

PART TWO
COMMON EXPERIENCES

EXTRA PAGES
If the lines in the individual exercise weren't enough, here is some more space for your stories

PART TWO
COMMON EXPERIENCES

PART TWO
COMMON EXPERIENCES

PART TWO
COMMON EXPERIENCES

PART TWO
COMMON EXPERIENCES

PART TWO

COMMON EXPERIENCES

Chapter Four
TURNING POINTS

Now that you have worked through some of the most basic prompts, let's go a little deeper.

Our lives are filled with Turning Points – the end of one chapter, the beginning of another. These life-changing moments are packed with stories – this is obvious. What may *not* be obvious is how to effectively procure relatable stories from these important experiences instead of just giving an overview of a big event.

That is one of the challenges with Turning Point stories (stories from the big moments in our life); it is easy to go too big, too general. We remember the overall emotion, the overall outcome, while the smaller snapshots get lost in the blur. However, it is the smaller pieces that offer the most points of connection with our audience. It's the smaller pieces that make it real and give it depth.

The following exercise is designed to shift your thinking – to focus on the smaller details of a big happening. As you think of each of the Turning Points listed below, I want you to try to think of individual moments, unseen fragments, specific emotions (fear, joy). Examining these big events on a micro-scale is a secret of the most skilled storytellers. It is in these details that the *true* story hides.

BIRTH OF A CHILD
First, give an overview of the event (write the story as you usually tell it):

....
....
....
....
....
....
....
....

PART TWO
TURNING POINTS

PART TWO
TURNING POINTS

Now. Let's break this event down a little.

During this event, was there a moment when you felt…

- ☐ Scared?
- ☐ Happy?
- ☐ Content?
- ☐ Vulnerable?
- ☐ ....
- ☐ Sad?
- ☐ Angry?
- ☐ Grateful?
- ☐ Empowered?
- ☐ ....
- ☐ Proud?
- ☐ Impressed?
- ☐ Inadequate?
- ☐ Embarrassed?
- ☐ ....

For each box you checked, describe the specific *moment* that made you feel that way.

Emotion #1 ....
....
....
....

Emotion #2 ....
....
....
....

Emotion #3 ....
....
....
....

Emotion #4 ....
....
....
....

Emotion #5 ....
....
....
....

Emotion #6 ....
....
....
....
....

PART TWO
TURNING POINTS

During this event, did you have any time to yourself? Or time that the other people participating in the overall event were not a part of?
What was on your mind in these moments?

....
....
....

Is there something about this event that you never told anyone (not necessarily because you were hiding it, but maybe because it just never came up)?

      Something that happened?
      Something you felt?
      Something you witnessed?

....
....
....
....
....
....
....

Anything else you remember about this event that you haven't typically shared:

....
....
....
....
....
....
....
....
....
....
....

PART TWO
TURNING POINTS

MARRIAGE PROPOSAL

First, give an overview of the event (write the story as you usually tell it):

PART TWO
TURNING POINTS

Time to break it down:

During this event, was there a moment when you felt…

- ☐ Scared?
- ☐ Happy?
- ☐ Content?
- ☐ Vulnerable?
- ☐ ....
- ☐ Sad?
- ☐ Angry?
- ☐ Grateful?
- ☐ Empowered?
- ☐ ....
- ☐ Proud?
- ☐ Impressed?
- ☐ Inadequate?
- ☐ Embarrassed?
- ☐ ....

For each box you checked, describe the specific *moment* that made you feel that way.

Emotion 1 ....
....
....
....

Emotion 2 ....
....
....
....

Emotion 3 ....
....
....
....

Emotion 4 ....
....
....
....

Emotion 5 ....
....
....
....

Emotion 6 ....
....
....
....

PART TWO
TURNING POINTS

During this event, did you have any time to yourself? Or time that the other people participating in the overall event were not a part of?
What was on your mind in these moments?

....
....
....

Is there something about this event that you never told anyone (not necessarily because you were hiding it, but maybe because it just never came up)?
      Something that happened?
      Something you felt?
      Something you witnessed?

....
....
....
....
....
....
....

Anything else you remember about this event that you haven't typically shared:

....
....
....
....
....
....
....
....
....
....

PART TWO
TURNING POINTS

YOUR WEDDING DAY

First, give an overview of the event (write the story as you usually tell it):

PART TWO
TURNING POINTS

Time to break it down.

During this event, was there a moment when you felt...

- ☐ Scared?
- ☐ Happy?
- ☐ Content?
- ☐ Vulnerable?
- ☐ ....
- ☐ Sad?
- ☐ Angry?
- ☐ Grateful?
- ☐ Empowered?
- ☐ ....
- ☐ Proud?
- ☐ Impressed?
- ☐ Inadequate?
- ☐ Embarrassed?
- ☐ ....

For each box you checked, describe the specific *moment* that made you feel that way.

Emotion 1 ....
....
....
....

Emotion 2 ....
....
....
....

Emotion 3 ....
....
....
....

Emotion 4 ....
....
....
....

Emotion 5 ....
....
....
....

Emotion 6 ....
....
....
....

PART TWO
TURNING POINTS

During this event, did you have any time to yourself? Or time that the other people participating in the overall event were not a part of?
What was on your mind in these moments?

Is there something about this event that you never told anyone (not necessarily because you were hiding it, but maybe because it just never came up)?

      Something that happened?
      Something you felt?
      Something you witnessed?

Anything else you remember about this event that you haven't typically shared:

PART TWO
TURNING POINTS

THE DAY YOU DECIDED (OR WERE TOLD) TO GET DIVORCED
First, give an overview of the event (write the story as you usually tell it):

PART TWO
TURNING POINTS

Time to break it down.

During this event, was there a moment when you felt...

- ☐ Scared?
- ☐ Happy?
- ☐ Content?
- ☐ Vulnerable?
- ☐ ....
- ☐ Sad?
- ☐ Angry?
- ☐ Grateful?
- ☐ Empowered?
- ☐ ....
- ☐ Proud?
- ☐ Impressed?
- ☐ Inadequate?
- ☐ Embarrassed?
- ☐ ....

For each box you checked, describe the specific *moment* that made you feel that way.

Emotion 1 ....
....
....
....

Emotion 2 ....
....
....
....

Emotion 3 ....
....
....
....

Emotion 4 ....
....
....
....

Emotion 5 ....
....
....
....

Emotion 6 ....
....
....
....

PART TWO
TURNING POINTS

During this event, did you have any time to yourself? Or time that the other people participating in the overall event were not a part of?
What was on your mind in these moments?

....
....
....

Is there something about this event that you never told anyone (not necessarily because you were hiding it, but maybe because it just never came up)?
    Something that happened?
    Something you felt?
    Something you witnessed?

....
....
....
....
....
....
....

Anything else you remember about this event that you haven't typically shared:

....
....
....
....
....
....
....
....
....
....

PART TWO
TURNING POINTS

THE DEATH OF A LOVED ONE
First, give an overview of the event (write the story as you usually tell it):

PART TWO
TURNING POINTS

Time to break it down.

During this event, was there a moment when you felt…

- ☐ Scared?
- ☐ Happy?
- ☐ Content?
- ☐ Vulnerable?
- ☐ ....
- ☐ Sad?
- ☐ Angry?
- ☐ Grateful?
- ☐ Empowered?
- ☐ ....
- ☐ Proud?
- ☐ Impressed?
- ☐ Inadequate?
- ☐ Embarrassed?
- ☐ ....

For each box you checked, describe the specific *moment* that made you feel that way.

Emotion 1 ....

Emotion 2 ....

Emotion 3 ....

Emotion 4 ....

Emotion 5 ....

Emotion 6 ....

PART TWO
TURNING POINTS

During this event, did you have any time to yourself? Or time that the other people participating in the overall event were not a part of?
What was on your mind in these moments?

....
....
....

Is there something about this event that you never told anyone (not necessarily because you were hiding it, but maybe because it just never came up)?

    Something that happened?
    Something you felt?
    Something you witnessed?

....
....
....
....
....
....
....
....

Anything else you remember about this event that you haven't typically shared:

....
....
....
....
....
....
....
....
....
....
....
....

PART TWO

TURNING POINTS

GOING TO COLLEGE

First, give an overview of the event (write the story as you usually tell it):

PART TWO
TURNING POINTS

Time to break it down.

During this event, was there a moment when you felt…
- ☐ Scared?   ☐ Happy?   ☐ Content?   ☐ Vulnerable?   ☐ ....
- ☐ Sad?   ☐ Angry?   ☐ Grateful?   ☐ Empowered?   ☐ ....
- ☐ Proud?   ☐ Impressed? ☐ Inadequate? ☐ Embarrassed? ☐ ....

For each box you checked, describe the specific *moment* that made you feel that way.

Emotion 1 ....
....
....
....

Emotion 2 ....
....
....
....

Emotion 3 ....
....
....
....

Emotion 4 ....
....
....
....

Emotion 5 ....
....
....
....

Emotion 6 ....
....
....
....

PART TWO
TURNING POINTS

During this event, did you have any time to yourself? Or time that the other people participating in the overall event were not a part of?
What was on your mind in these moments?

....
....
....

Is there something about this event that you never told anyone (not necessarily because you were hiding it, but maybe because it just never came up)?

    Something that happened?
    Something you felt?
    Something you witnessed?

....
....
....
....
....
....
....

Anything else you remember about this event that you haven't typically shared:

....
....
....
....
....
....
....
....
....
....
....

PART TWO
TURNING POINTS

PURCHASED YOUR FIRST HOME

First, give an overview of the event (write the story as you usually tell it):

PART TWO
TURNING POINTS

Time to break it down.

During this event, was there a moment when you felt…

- ☐ Scared?
- ☐ Happy?
- ☐ Content?
- ☐ Vulnerable?
- ☐ ....
- ☐ Sad?
- ☐ Angry?
- ☐ Grateful?
- ☐ Empowered?
- ☐ ....
- ☐ Proud?
- ☐ Impressed?
- ☐ Inadequate?
- ☐ Embarrassed?
- ☐ ....

For each box you checked, describe the specific *moment* that made you feel that way.

Emotion 1 ....
....
....
....

Emotion 2 ....
....
....
....

Emotion 3 ....
....
....
....

Emotion 4 ....
....
....
....

Emotion 5 ....
....
....
....

Emotion 6 ....
....
....
....

PART TWO
TURNING POINTS

During this event, did you have any time to yourself? Or time that the other people participating in the overall event were not a part of?
What was on your mind in these moments?

....
....
....

Is there something about this event that you never told anyone (not necessarily because you were hiding it, but maybe because it just never came up)?

      Something that happened?
      Something you felt?
      Something you witnessed?

....
....
....
....
....
....
....

Anything else you remember about this event that you haven't typically shared:

....
....
....
....
....
....
....
....
....
....
....
....

PART TWO
TURNING POINTS

I understand that some of these Turning Points are not relevant to you – and that there are others I haven't included that *are* relevant. Use the following pages to identify a few of your *own* Turning Points and answer the same questions. Remember, the goal is to identify the smaller moments that make these big experiences unique and memorable.

TURNING POINT 1

First, give an overview of the event (write the story as you usually tell it):

PART TWO
TURNING POINTS

Time to break it down.

During this event, was there a moment when you felt…

- ☐ Scared?
- ☐ Happy?
- ☐ Content?
- ☐ Vulnerable?
- ☐ ....
- ☐ Sad?
- ☐ Angry?
- ☐ Grateful?
- ☐ Empowered?
- ☐ ....
- ☐ Proud?
- ☐ Impressed?
- ☐ Inadequate?
- ☐ Embarrassed?
- ☐ ....

For each box you checked, describe the specific *moment* that made you feel that way.

Emotion 1 ....
....
....

Emotion 2 ....
....
....

Emotion 3 ....
....
....

Emotion 4 ....
....
....

Emotion 5 ....
....
....

Emotion 6 ....
....
....
....

PART TWO
TURNING POINTS

During this event, did you have any time to yourself? Or time that the other people participating in the overall event were not a part of?

What was on your mind in these moments?

....
....
....

Is there something about this event that you never told anyone (not necessarily because you were hiding it, but maybe because it just never came up)?

    Something that happened?
    Something you felt?
    Something you witnessed?

....
....
....
....
....
....
....

Anything else you remember about this event that you haven't typically shared:

....
....
....
....
....
....
....
....
....
....
....

PART TWO
TURNING POINTS

TURNING POINT 2

First, give an overview of the event (write the story as you usually tell it):

PART TWO
TURNING POINTS

Time to break it down.

During this event, was there a moment when you felt…

☐ Scared?   ☐ Happy?   ☐ Content?   ☐ Vulnerable?   ☐ ....
☐ Sad?   ☐ Angry?   ☐ Grateful? ☐ Empowered?   ☐ ....
☐ Proud?   ☐ Impressed? ☐ Inadequate? ☐ Embarrassed? ☐ ....

For each box you checked, describe the specific *moment* that made you feel that way.

Emotion 1 ....
....
....
....

Emotion 2 ....
....
....
....

Emotion 3 ....
....
....
....

Emotion 4 ....
....
....
....

Emotion 5 ....
....
....
....

Emotion 6 ....
....
....
....

PART TWO
TURNING POINTS

During this event, did you have any time to yourself? Or time that the other people participating in the overall event were not a part of?
What was on your mind in these moments?

....
....
....

Is there something about this event that you never told anyone (not necessarily because you were hiding it, but maybe because it just never came up)?
    Something that happened?
    Something you felt?
    Something you witnessed?

....
....
....
....
....
....
....
....

Anything else you remember about this event that you haven't typically shared:

....
....
....
....
....
....
....
....
....
....
....

PART TWO
TURNING POINTS

TURNING POINT 3

First, give an overview of the event (write the story as you usually tell it):

PART TWO
TURNING POINTS

Time to break it down.

During this event, was there a moment when you felt…

☐ Scared? ☐ Happy? ☐ Content? ☐ Vulnerable? ☐ ....
☐ Sad?   ☐ Angry? ☐ Grateful? ☐ Empowered?   ☐ ....
☐ Proud?   ☐ Impressed? ☐ Inadequate? ☐ Embarrassed? ☐ ....

For each box you checked, describe the specific *moment* that made you feel that way.

Emotion 1 ....
....
....
....

Emotion 2 ....
....
....
....

Emotion 3 ....
....
....
....

Emotion 4 ....
....
....
....

Emotion 5 ....
....
....
....

Emotion 6 ....
....
....
....

PART TWO
TURNING POINTS

During this event, did you have any time to yourself? Or time that the other people participating in the overall event were not a part of?

What was on your mind in these moments?

....
....
....

Is there something about this event that you never told anyone (not necessarily because you were hiding it, but maybe because it just never came up)?

      Something that happened?

      Something you felt?

      Something you witnessed?

....
....
....
....
....
....
....

Anything else you remember about this event that you haven't typically shared:

....
....
....
....
....
....
....
....
....
....
....
....

PART TWO
TURNING POINTS

TURNING POINT 4

First, give an overview of the event (write the story as you usually tell it):

PART TWO
TURNING POINTS

Time to break it down.

During this event, was there a moment when you felt...

- ☐ Scared?
- ☐ Happy?
- ☐ Content?
- ☐ Vulnerable?
- ☐ ....
- ☐ Sad?
- ☐ Angry?
- ☐ Grateful?
- ☐ Empowered?
- ☐ ....
- ☐ Proud?
- ☐ Impressed?
- ☐ Inadequate?
- ☐ Embarrassed?
- ☐ ....

For each box you checked, describe the specific *moment* that made you feel that way.

Emotion 1 ....
....
....
....

Emotion 2 ....
....
....
....

Emotion 3 ....
....
....
....

Emotion 4 ....
....
....
....

Emotion 5 ....
....
....
....

Emotion 6 ....
....
....
....

PART TWO
TURNING POINTS

During this event, did you have any time to yourself? Or time that the other people participating in the overall event were not a part of?
What was on your mind in these moments?

....
....
....

Is there something about this event that you never told anyone (not necessarily because you were hiding it, but maybe because it just never came up)?
    Something that happened?
    Something you felt?
    Something you witnessed?

....
....
....
....
....
....
....

Anything else you remember about this event that you haven't typically shared:

....
....
....
....
....
....
....
....
....
....
....
....

PART TWO
TURNING POINTS

EXTRA PAGES
If the lines in the individual exercise weren't enough, here is some more space for your stories

PART TWO
TURNING POINTS

PART TWO
TURNING POINTS

PART TWO
TURNING POINTS

PART TWO
TURNING POINTS

PART TWO
TURNING POINTS

Chapter Five
CREATING LISTS

The following story-finding strategy is the most thorough of any outlined in this book. Creating lists is designed to target all aspects, layers, and levels of your life. By identifying very basic people, places, and things in your life you also unlock the memories (and subsequently, the stories) associated *with* these people, places, and things. We're going to take this process down in four phases, gradually getting more difficult as we go.

When I was in first grade, my parents built a house on a 10-acre piece of land in the middle of nowhere. Which meant my bus ride (arguably the WORST part of any school day) was an hour long IF the weather was good, which, growing up in Minnesota, wasn't often.

I would pass the time by writing a single word in the center of a lined piece of paper, and then I would draw a line and write the very first word the previous one made me think of. Then another line to the next word I thought of. Another line. Another word. Another line. Not thinking, not analyzing; just moving from one word to the next until the entire page was filled with a web of connected words.

Then, and only then, I went back to the beginning and retraced my steps. I looked at the words and the lines that connected them and asked myself, "What made me think of that?" "Why were these two connected for me?" Each answer led to a memory, a small story, something that had been locked in my subconscious until I released it with a word. It was fascinating and made an unbearable bus ride home ALMOST enjoyable.

I know there are other ways to spend time on a school bus and there were certainly times when I did my homework, read a book, talked to my "bus-friends," or was defending myself against the inevitable

PART TWO
CREATING LISTS

bus-bully. But my favorite (and looking back, most productive) hours were spent accessing memories that had otherwise been buried.

Much like the words scribbled on a piece of paper on a bus ride home, these lists will help unlock your stories.

PHASE 1 - LIST CREATION

One of the challenges with finding your stories is the questions we ask ourselves as we begin our search. On the most basic level, our memories are attached to the people who were in them and the places they happened. Phase One of this exercise focuses on simply identifying the people and places in your life – people and places you probably haven't thought of in a while. As you write each item down, allow yourself a little room to think of the memories that are connected with each – *that* is where you will find your stories.

A few rules before you begin this exercise.

1. Be thorough and *work* at it. This is not a time to be lazy. There will likely be moments when you look at the prompt and think, "Eh, I don't really remember all of my teachers. It can't be that important, I'll skip it." I understand that there will be times when you need more time to recall, or times when, yes, the memory is simply gone. But if you find yourself "skimming the prompts" more than you're actually *doing* them, you're missing an incredible opportunity.

2. Have fun. It's not very often you can indulge in an extended trip down memory lane.

3. DO NOT listen to the voice inside your head that is telling you this exercise is pointless/silly/stupid. It might SEEM like a waste of time: Why spend any energy on things that are so insignificant? Why try to find details you won't use anyway? Instead, listen to THIS voice, MY voice, telling you:
First, you never know when a significant story will emerge.
If that's not good enough then,
Second, "insignificant details" are what give our stories depth. Whether or not you "use" all of the recollections in this section is not as important as the color they add to the bigger stories you will find. This is something we will discuss further in the next installment of this training series: **Crafting Your Story**. You will want to be prepared.

PHASE 1 PROMPTS
Every house you ever lived in

PART TWO
CREATING LISTS

Every teacher you ever had

....
....
....

Every professor

....
....
....

All of your aunts

....
....
....

All of your uncles

....
....
....

All of your grandparents

....
....

All of your cousins

....
....
....

Family vacations

....
....
....

PART TWO
CREATING LISTS

Sports you played

Sports you *tried* to play

People who were like family

Every car you owned

Best childhood friends

Best teenage friends

Best college friends

Best adult friends

PART TWO
CREATING LISTS

Your enemies (people you never liked/never liked you/had it in for)

....
....

Your crushes (people you liked from afar)

....
....

Your boyfriends/girlfriends (people you got to like up close)

....
....

Babysitters

....
....

People at your church

....
....
....

People you know/see at the gym

....
....

Your kids' friends

....
....

Your kids' friends' parents

....
....

PART TWO
CREATING LISTS

Jobs you had (big, small, summer, temporary, babysitting, dog walking, whatever)

....
....
....

Extracurricular activities you participated in (go all the way back – any after-school enrichment activity)

....
....
....

Places you traveled overseas

....
....

Classes you took in college

....
....
....
....

Pets (imaginary? real?)

....
....

Bosses

....
....

Coworkers (through out life)

....
....
....
....

PART TWO
CREATING LISTS

Family traditions

....
....
....

How did you celebrate... (go by year if you can)
   Valentine's Day?

....
....
....

   Christmas/Hanukah/Kwanza?

....
....
....

   New Year's?

....
....
....

   Halloween?

....
....

   Your birthday?

....
....
....

   Any holiday not on this list?

....
....

PART TWO
CREATING LISTS

Use these pages to create some of your own lists.

List 1

List 2

List 3

List 4

List 5

List 6

List 7

List 8

List 9

PART TWO
CREATING LISTS

List 10

List 11

List 12

List 13

List 14

List 15

List 16

List 17

List 18

List 19

PART TWO
CREATING LISTS

PHASE 2 - LIST EXPANSION

Now that you have recalled the most basic pieces of information (nouns), go back and do some additional work with each person/place/thing you wrote down. This is where we start filling in the blanks of your memory. I am going to give you two options for getting this done.

OPTION 1: QUESTION & ANSWER

Each item you wrote on that list has a history to it. Each item is housing stories. Getting to those stories requires a little digging. Here's how: Ask yourself the following questions then write down absolutely anything else you remember about each item on your list. Big or small, write it down.

For PLACES ask:

    Who would I see there?

    What would I do there?

    What is my best memory of that place? My worst memory?

For ACTIVITIES ask:

    Who was there with me?

    What did I enjoy about that activity? Or dislike?

    What is my best memory of that activity? My worst memory?

For PEOPLE ask:

    When/where did we meet?

    What was my first impression?

    What is something we did/do together?

    What stands out most about their physical appearance?

    What stands out most about their personality?

    What is my best memory of that person? My worst memory?

OPTION 2: MAKE A WEB

For some people, a list just isn't going to get it done. You need something a little bit more organic, something that allows a little more mental space for the memories to come to you. If that is you, use the webs to expand the items on your previous lists. Here is where the concept of the "webs" from my bus ride home is helpful.

Start by writing an item from one of your lists in the center of the circle. Then write down the first four things that come to mind when thinking about that item. On the lines provided, make a quick note of *WHY* you thought of that. Then expand *again,* this time by writing three more "words that come to mind" for each of the previous four. Use any remaining space on the page to write why *those* words came to mind. More than anything, just sit back and see where the web takes you.

PART TWO
CREATING LISTS

PHASE 2: OPTION 1 – QUESTION & ANSWER

1. List Item: .... Item Type: (circle one) Place Activity Person

Question: ....

Answer:

....
....
....
....
....
....
....
....
....
....
....
....
....

Question: ....

Answer:

....
....
....
....
....
....
....
....
....
....
....
....
....

PART TWO
CREATING LISTS

PHASE 2: OPTION 2 - MAKE A WEB

List Item

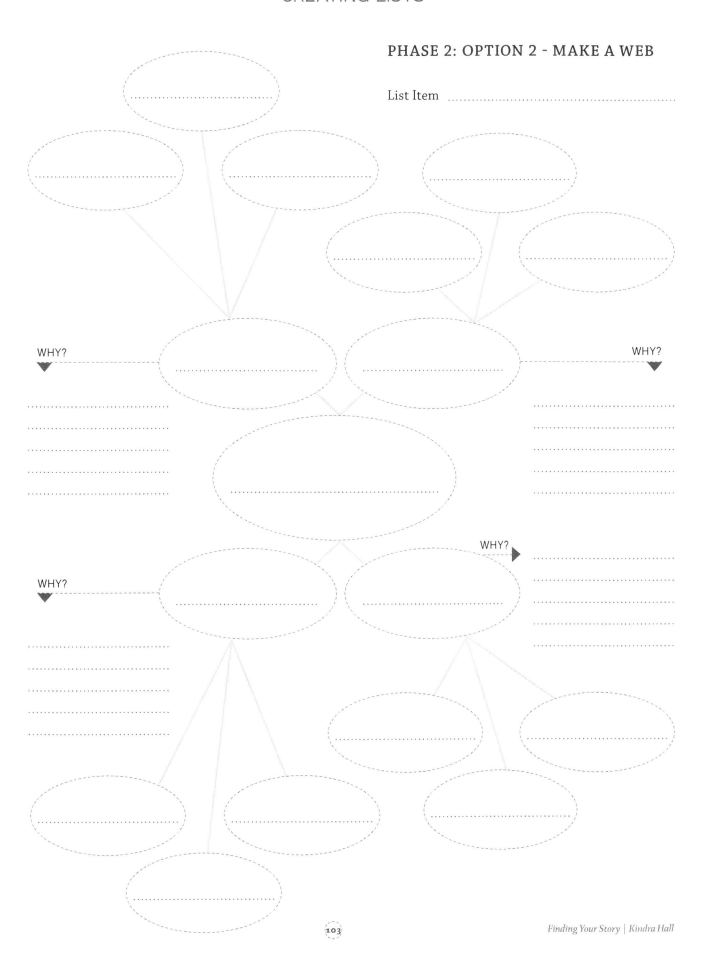

PART TWO
CREATING LISTS

2. List Item: .... Item Type: (circle one) Place Activity Person

Question: ....

Answer:

....
....
....
....
....
....
....
....
....
....
....
....
....
....

Question: ....

Answer:

....
....
....
....
....
....
....
....
....
....
....
....
....
....

PART TWO
CREATING LISTS

List Item ....

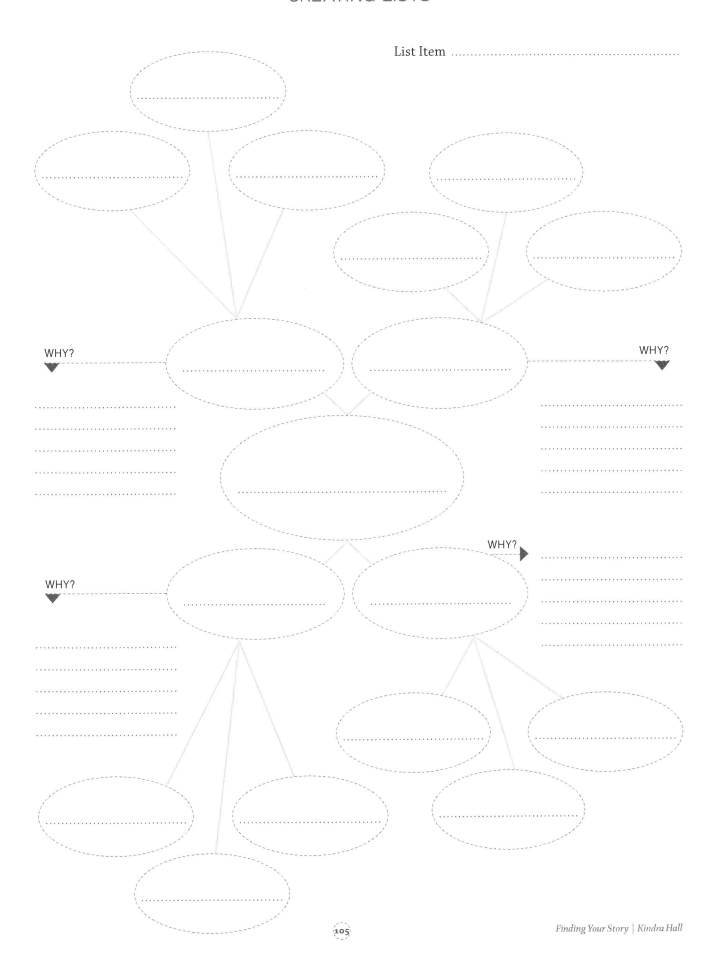

PART TWO
CREATING LISTS

3. List Item: .... Item Type: (circle one) Place Activity Person

Question: ....

Answer:

....
....
....
....
....
....
....
....
....
....
....
....
....
....

Question: ....

Answer:

....
....
....
....
....
....
....
....
....
....
....
....
....
....

PART TWO
CREATING LISTS

List Item ....

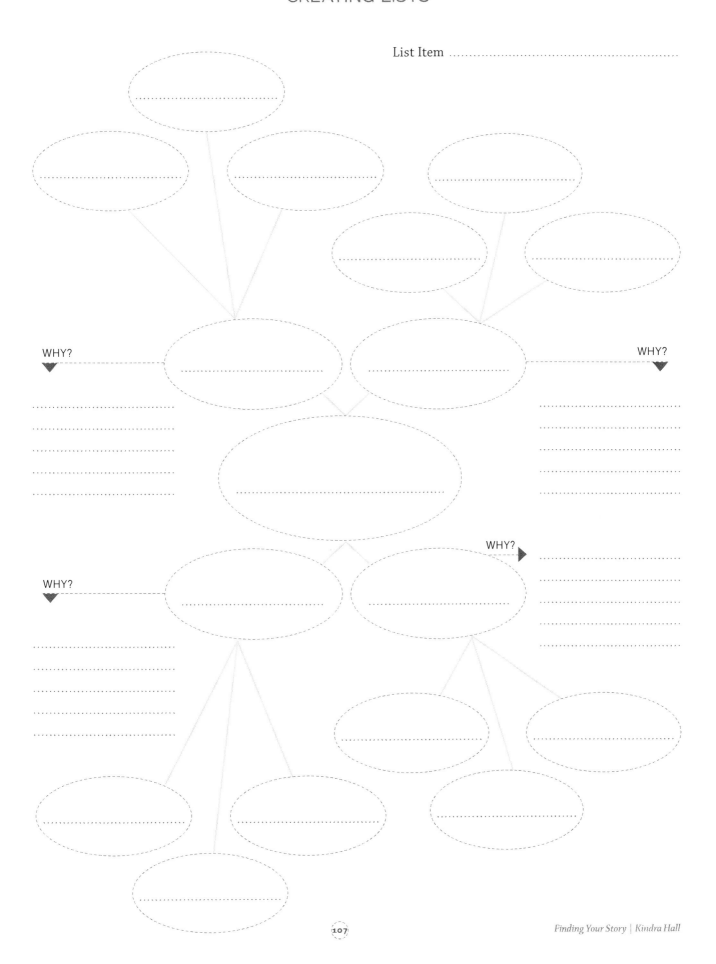

PART TWO
CREATING LISTS

4. List Item: .... Item Type: (circle one) Place Activity Person

Question: ....

Answer:

....
....
....
....
....
....
....
....
....
....
....
....
....
....

Question: ....

Answer:

....
....
....
....
....
....
....
....
....
....
....
....
....
....

PART TWO
CREATING LISTS

List Item ....

PART TWO
CREATING LISTS

5. List Item: .... Item Type: (circle one) Place Activity Person

Question: ....

Answer:

....
....
....
....
....
....
....
....
....
....
....
....
....

Question: ....

Answer:

....
....
....
....
....
....
....
....
....
....
....
....
....

PART TWO
CREATING LISTS

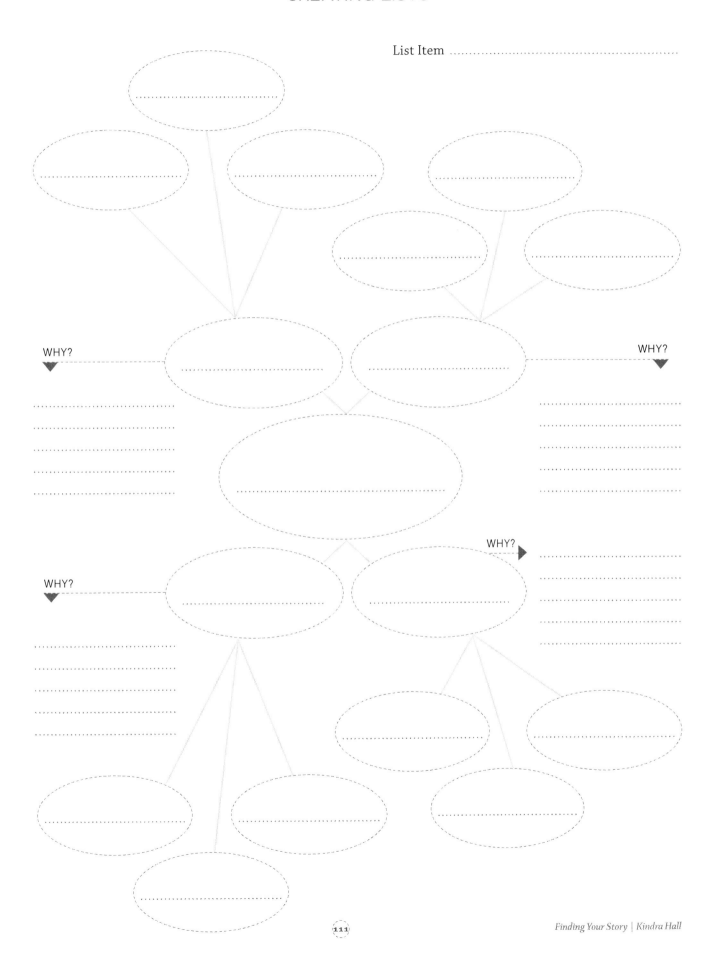

PART TWO
CREATING LISTS

6. List Item: .... Item Type: (circle one) Place Activity Person

Question: ....

Answer:

....
....
....
....
....
....
....
....
....
....
....
....
....

Question: ....

Answer:

....
....
....
....
....
....
....
....
....
....
....
....
....

PART TWO
CREATING LISTS

List Item ....

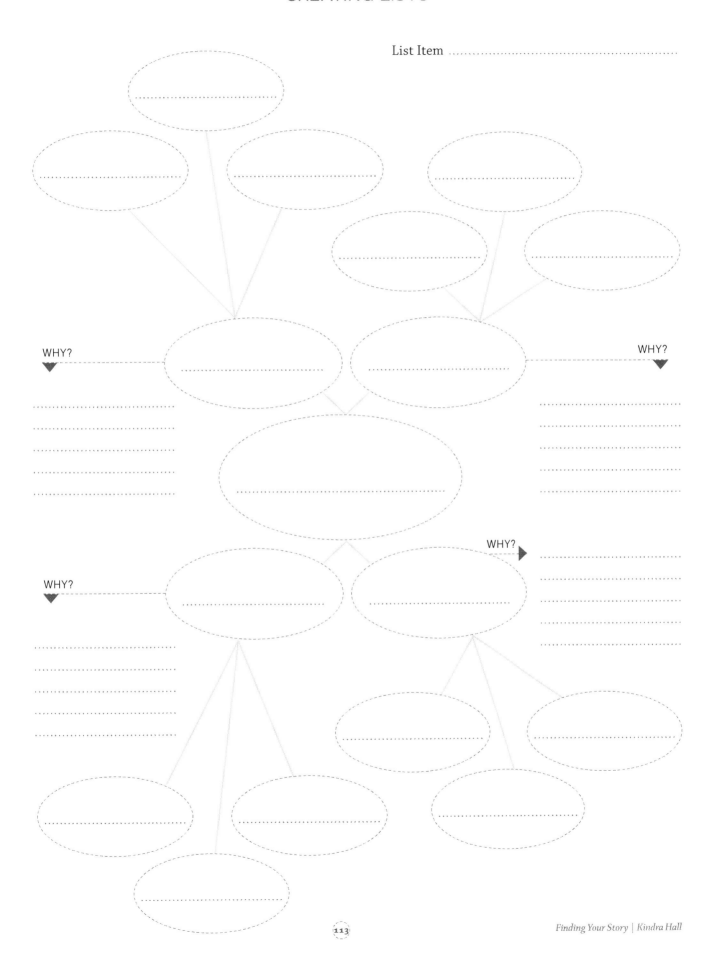

PART TWO
CREATING LISTS

7. List Item: .... Item Type: (circle one) Place Activity Person

Question: ....

Answer:

....
....
....
....
....
....
....
....
....
....
....
....
....

Question: ....

Answer:

....
....
....
....
....
....
....
....
....
....
....
....
....

PART TWO
CREATING LISTS

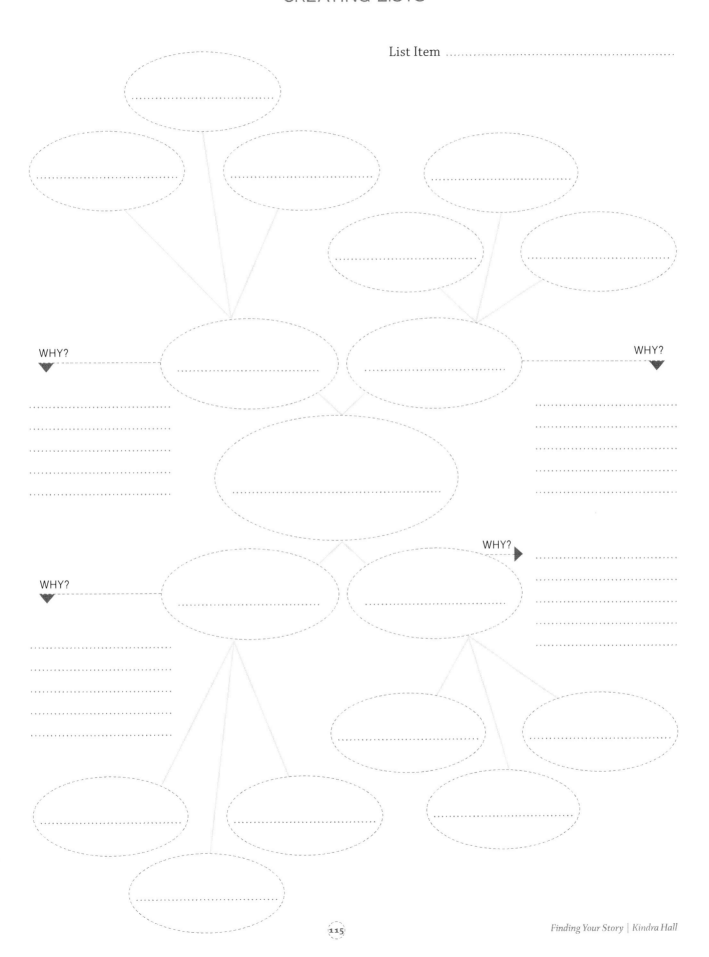

PART TWO
CREATING LISTS

8. List Item: .... Item Type: (circle one) Place Activity Person

Question: ....

Answer:

....
....
....
....
....
....
....
....
....
....
....
....
....
....

Question: ....

Answer:

....
....
....
....
....
....
....
....
....
....
....
....
....
....

PART TWO
CREATING LISTS

List Item ....

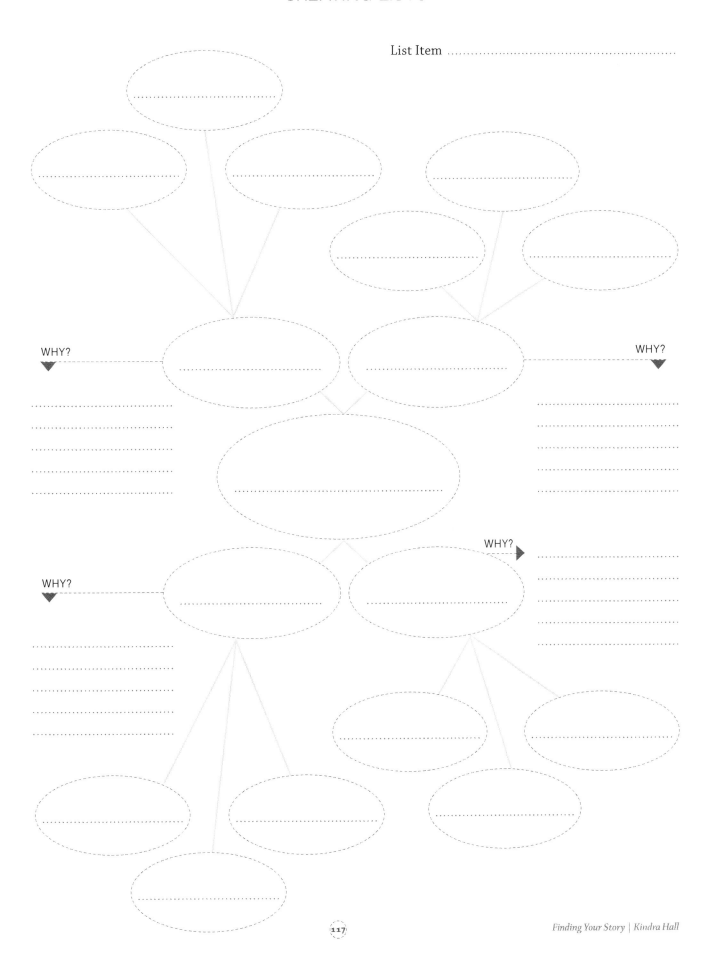

PART TWO
CREATING LISTS

9. List Item: .... Item Type: (circle one) Place Activity Person

Question: ....

Answer:

....
....
....
....
....
....
....
....
....
....
....
....
....

Question: ....

Answer:

....
....
....
....
....
....
....
....
....
....
....
....
....

PART TWO
CREATING LISTS

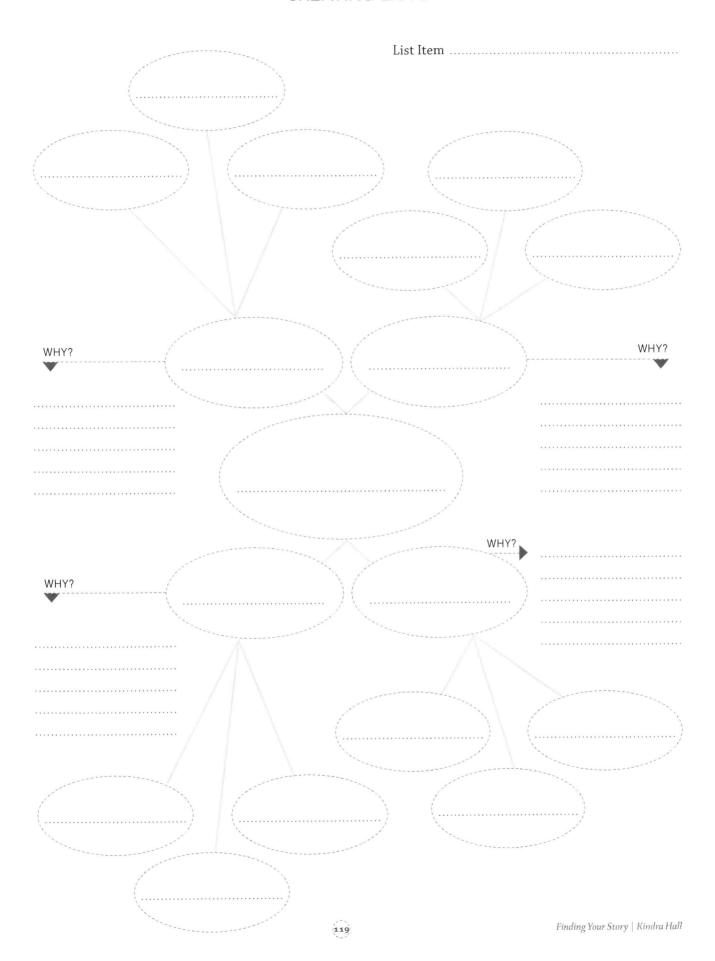

PART TWO
CREATING LISTS

10. List Item: .... Item Type: (circle one) Place Activity Person

Question: ....

Answer:

....
....
....
....
....
....
....
....
....
....
....
....

Question: ....

Answer:

....
....
....
....
....
....
....
....
....
....
....
....

PART TWO
CREATING LISTS

List Item ....

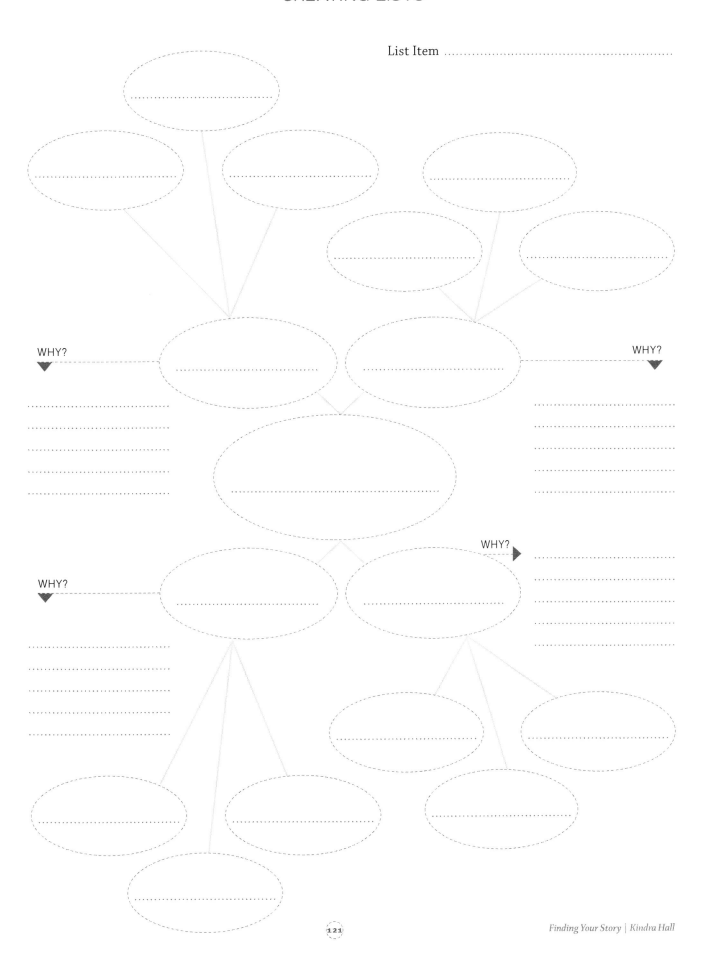

PART TWO
CREATING LISTS

11. List Item: .... Item Type: (circle one) Place Activity Person

Question: ....

Answer:

....
....
....
....
....
....
....
....
....
....
....
....
....

Question: ....

Answer:

....
....
....
....
....
....
....
....
....
....
....
....
....

PART TWO
CREATING LISTS

PART TWO
CREATING LISTS

12. List Item: .... Item Type: (circle one) Place Activity Person

Question: ....

Answer:

....
....
....
....
....
....
....
....
....
....
....
....

Question: ....

Answer:

....
....
....
....
....
....
....
....
....
....
....
....

PART TWO
CREATING LISTS

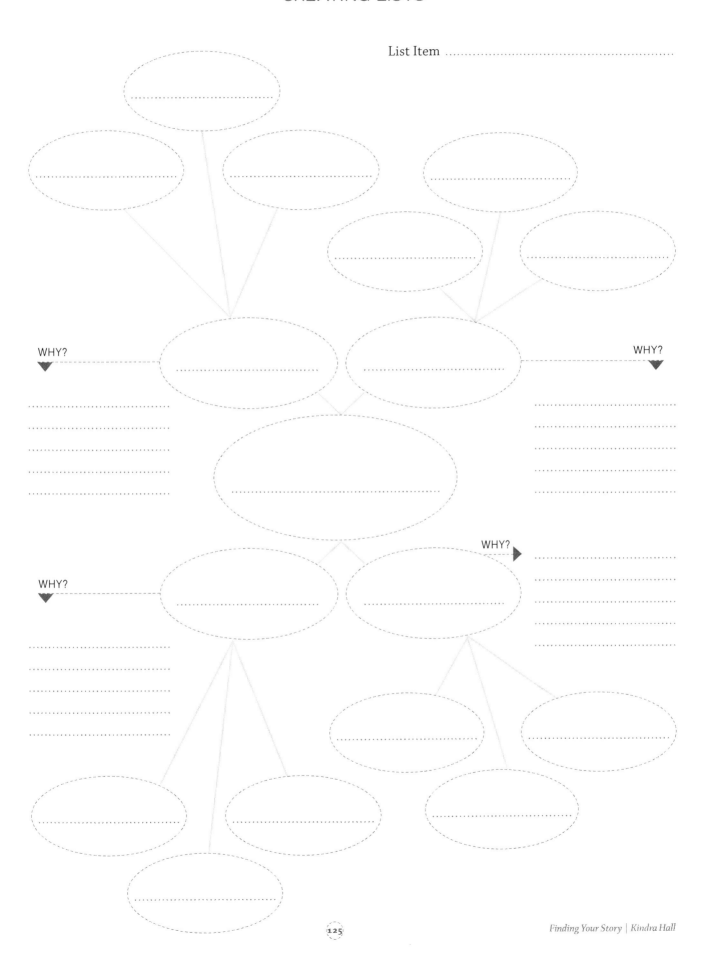

PART TWO
CREATING LISTS

13. List Item: .... Item Type: (circle one) Place Activity Person

Question: ....

Answer:

....
....
....
....
....
....
....
....
....
....
....
....
....

Question: ....

Answer:

....
....
....
....
....
....
....
....
....
....
....
....
....

PART TWO
CREATING LISTS

List Item ....

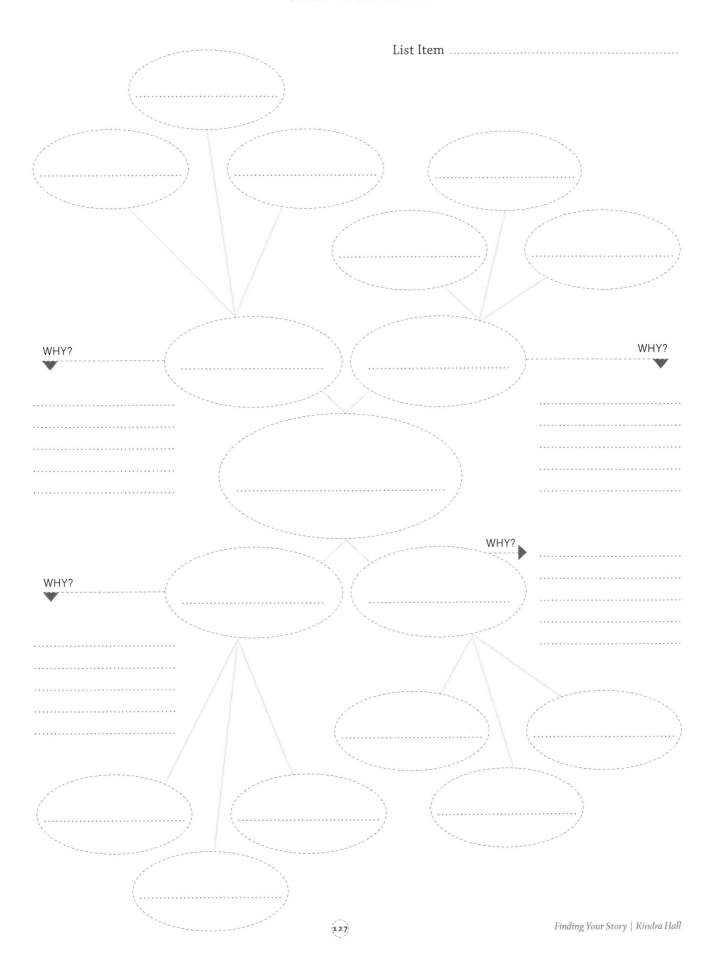

PART TWO
CREATING LISTS

14. List Item: .... Item Type: (circle one) Place Activity Person

Question: ....

Answer:

Question: ....

Answer:

PART TWO
CREATING LISTS

List Item ....

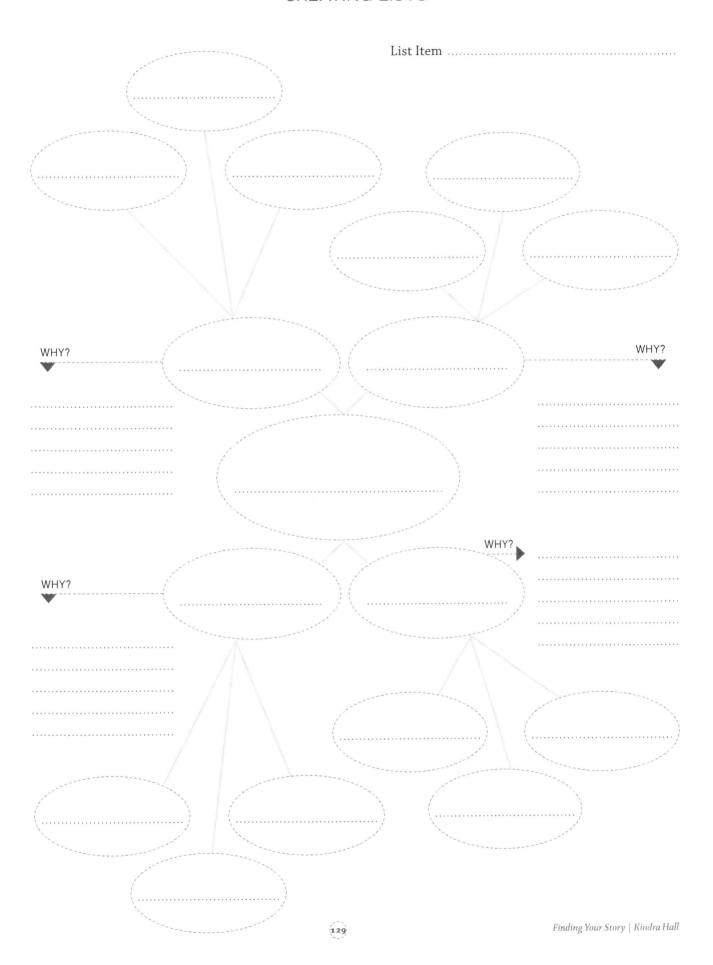

PART TWO
CREATING LISTS

15. List Item: .... Item Type: (circle one) Place Activity Person

Question: ....

Answer:

....
....
....
....
....
....
....
....
....
....
....
....
....

Question: ....

Answer:

....
....
....
....
....
....
....
....
....
....
....
....
....

PART TWO
CREATING LISTS

List Item ....

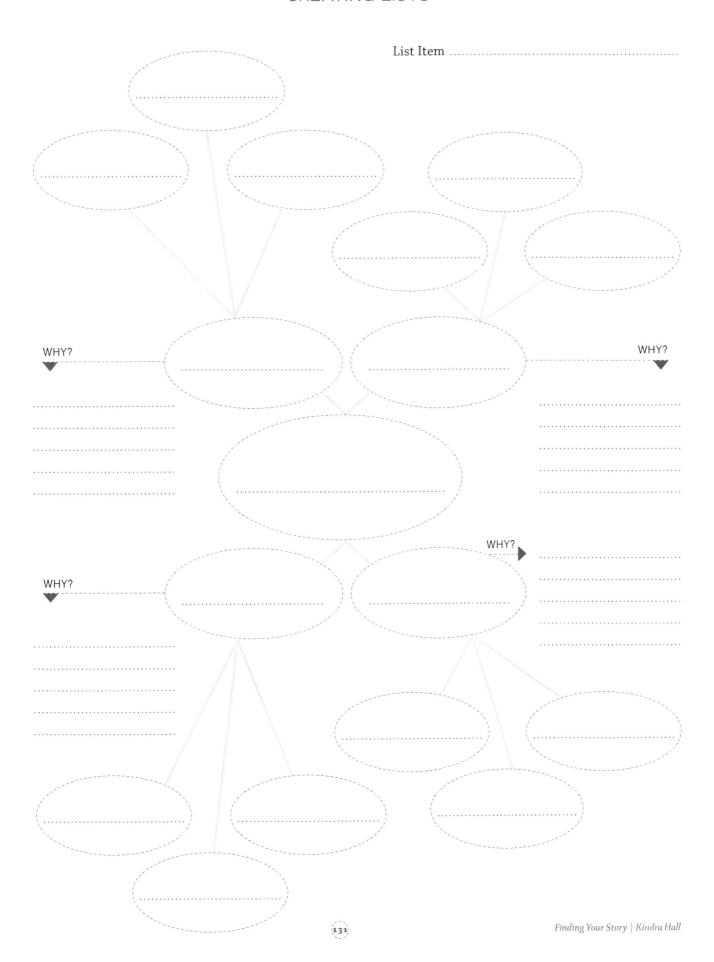

PART TWO
CREATING LISTS

16. List Item: .... Item Type: (circle one) Place Activity Person

Question: ....

Answer:

....
....
....
....
....
....
....
....
....
....
....
....

Question: ....

Answer:

....
....
....
....
....
....
....
....
....
....
....
....

PART TWO
CREATING LISTS

List Item ....

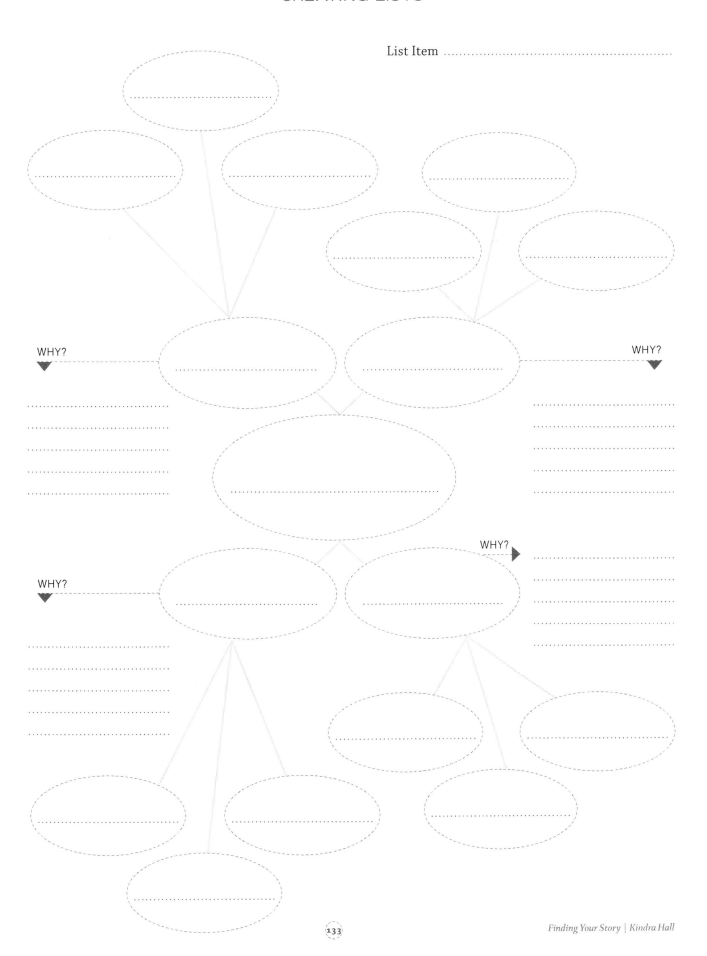

PART TWO
CREATING LISTS

17. List Item: .... Item Type: (circle one) Place Activity Person

Question: ....

Answer:

....
....
....
....
....
....
....
....
....
....
....
....
....
....

Question: ....

Answer:

....
....
....
....
....
....
....
....
....
....
....
....
....
....

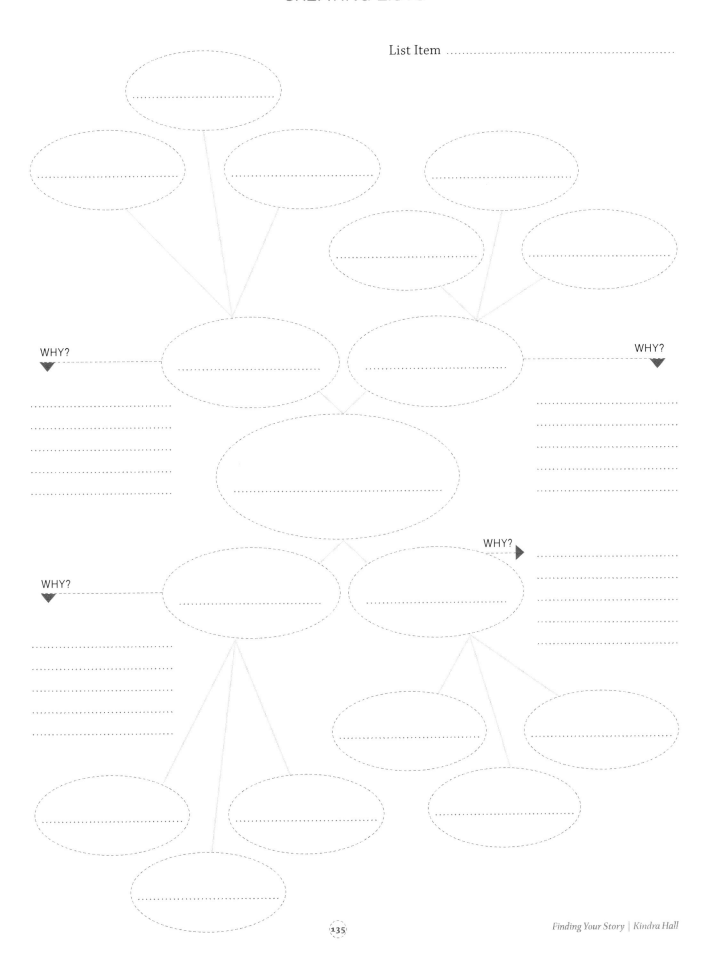

PART TWO
CREATING LISTS

18. List Item: .... Item Type: (circle one) Place Activity Person

Question: ....

Answer:

....
....
....
....
....
....
....
....
....
....
....
....

Question: ....

Answer:

....
....
....
....
....
....
....
....
....
....
....
....

PART TWO
CREATING LISTS

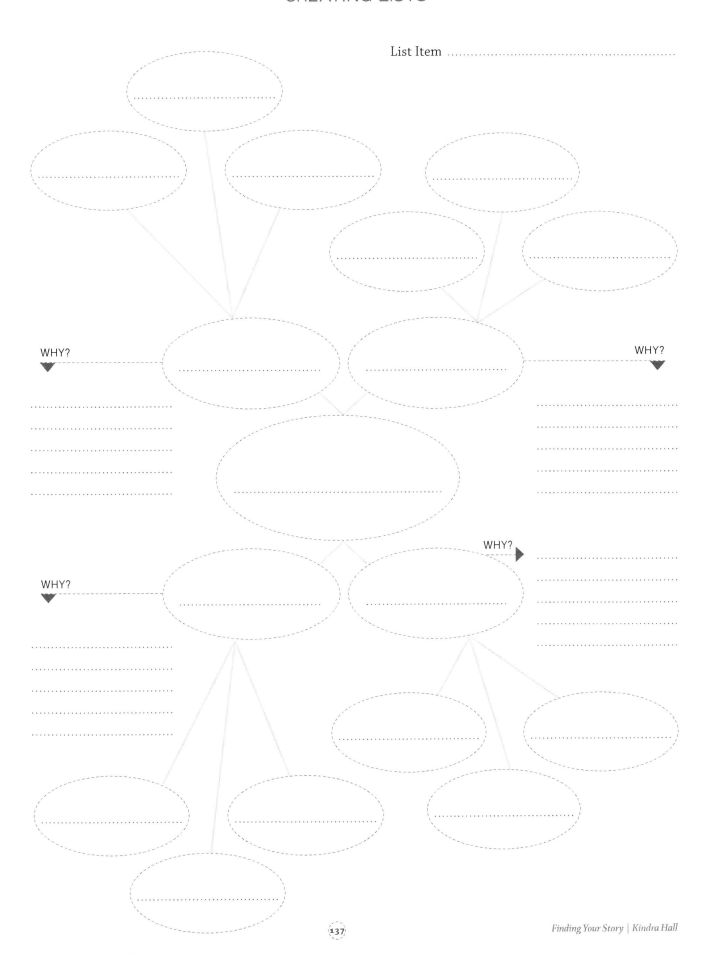

PART TWO
CREATING LISTS

19. List Item: .... Item Type: (circle one) Place Activity Person

Question: ....

Answer:

Question: ....

Answer:

PART TWO
CREATING LISTS

List Item ....

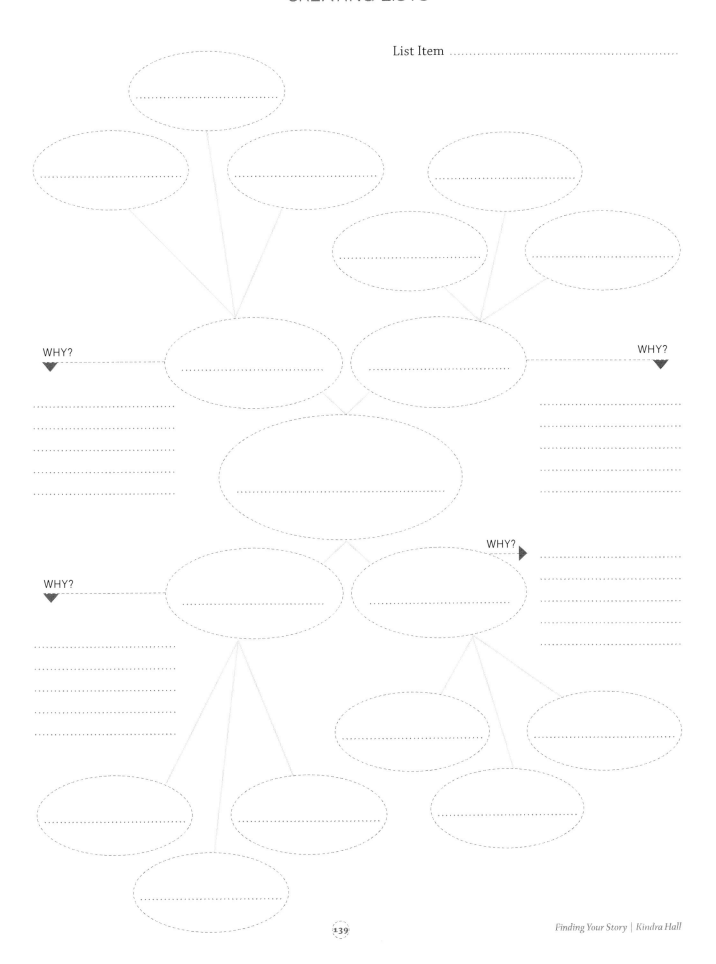

PART TWO
CREATING LISTS

20. List Item: .... Item Type: (circle one) Place Activity Person

Question: ....

Answer:

Question: ....

Answer:

PART TWO
CREATING LISTS

PART TWO
CREATING LISTS

PHASE 3 - EMOTIONAL EVENTS

This third phase of creating lists is a little more advanced. It requires you to recall specific events or in some cases it requires you to recall specific emotions. This isn't how our memory organizes things, which makes accessing the stories via these kinds of prompts more challenging. However, by completing Phase 1 and 2, some of these events or emotions are closer to the surface and therefore easier to capture.

YOUR BIGGEST FIGHTS

With a friend:

1.

2.

3.

4.

With a family member:

1.

PART TWO
CREATING LISTS

2. ....

3. ....

4. ....

In a romantic relationship:

1. ....

2. ....

3. ....

4. ....

PART TWO
CREATING LISTS

In a professional relationship:

1.

2.

3.

4.

TIMES YOU'VE BEEN SCARED

1.

2.

PART TWO
CREATING LISTS

3.

4.

TIMES YOU'VE DONE SOMETHING NICE FOR SOMEONE

1.

2.

3.

4.

PART TWO
CREATING LISTS

TIMES YOU'VE FELT SPECIAL

1. ....
   ....
   ....
   ....
   ....

2. ....
   ....
   ....
   ....
   ....

3. ....
   ....
   ....
   ....
   ....

4. ....
   ....
   ....
   ....
   ....

YOUR PROUDEST MOMENTS

1. ....
   ....
   ....
   ....
   ....

2. ....
   ....
   ....
   ....
   ....

PART TWO
CREATING LISTS

3. ....
   ....
   ....
   ....
   ....

4. ....
   ....
   ....
   ....
   ....

PART TWO
CREATING LISTS

PHASE 4 - OUT OF CHARACTER

This is the final phase of this chapter. This phase requires an elevated state of self-awareness. I am going to ask you to first identify the kind of person you *are* and then identify a time when you reacted out of character. Interesting stories happen when we do something or behave in a way that is not our norm.

If you're NOT the kind of person who cries...
    List the times you HAVE cried.

....
....
....
....
....

    Choose one and tell me more:

....
....
....
....
....
....
....

If you're NOT the kind of person who falls in love...
    List the times you've been in love.

....
....
....
....
....

    Choose one and tell me more:

....
....
....
....
....
....
....

PART TWO
CREATING LISTS

If you're NOT the kind of person who is ever late…
　　List the times you've been late.

....
....
....
....
....

　　Choose one and tell me more:

....
....
....
....

If you're not the kind of person who takes risks…
　　What are the riskiest things you've ever done?

....
....
....
....
....

　　Choose one and tell me more:

....
....
....
....

If you're NOT the kind of person who acts spontaneously…
　　What are the most spontaneous things you've ever done?

....
....
....
....

PART TWO
CREATING LISTS

Choose one and tell me more:

....
....
....
....
....

If you are NOT the kind of person who likes confrontation...
　　List the times you confronted someone, or someone confronted you?

....
....
....
....
....

Choose one and tell me more:

....
....
....
....
....
....

PART TWO
CREATING LISTS

EXTRA PAGES
If the lines in the individual exercise weren't enough, here is some more space for your stories

PART TWO
CREATING LISTS

PART TWO
CREATING LISTS

Chapter Six
TRIGGERS

> **INFORMATION HITS THE MIND; STORY HITS THE HEART.**
> – PETER GUBER

Some things have the amazing ability to act as time machines. All it takes is a song, a smell, a bite of bread pudding that tastes just like my grandmother's and I am transported to another time, another place. Items like these are like these are triggers - triggering memories that otherwise remain trapped and inaccessible. These "time machine" touch points are a great tool when looking for personal stories. Most of the time they occur spontaneously; however, you can encourage them. Below are Trigger Exercises. Use each one of these Trigger tools to access memories that are hiding behind the passage of time so they can become stories.

MUSIC

Just this past Wednesday night I was taking a spin class and the instructor played a remixed version of a song that had been popular just as I was graduating high school ("Truly, Madly, Deeply," to be exact). As the chorus came on, the girl riding next to me leaned over and said with a sigh that was not exercise related. "Oh! This was my song with my high school boyfriend…." As we rode in the dark I could tell she wore a slight smile on her face, perhaps remembering the story of a sweet memory.

It only takes one bar of music to send us back 20 years and refresh the fine details of a time that has long since passed. In this way, music acts as a Trigger. Go online and find the Top 100 List from a specific year: your high school graduation, when you started dating your spouse. Listen to a few of the songs. As each song plays, write down any images or memories that come to mind.

PART TWO
TRIGGERS

Song 1
Title: ....
Memories:

Song 2
Title: ....
Memories:

PART TWO
TRIGGERS

Song 3
Title: ....
Memories:

Song 4
Title: ....
Memories:

PART TWO
TRIGGERS

Song 5
Title: ....
Memories:

....
....
....
....
....
....
....
....
....
....
....
....
....
....

Song 6
Title: ....
Memories:

....
....
....
....
....
....
....
....
....
....
....
....
....
....

PART TWO
TRIGGERS

PHOTOGRAPHS

Photographs are a great Trigger tool. By default they capture moments of memories – a moment is all you need to find a story. Go to where you keep your old photographs (an album, a box, an envelope, a yearbook). Thumb through them and choose a handful to complete the following exercises.

Photo 1

Who is in the photo? How do you know them?
      When was the photo taken?
      Where were you?
      Why were you there?
      What was happening when that photo was taken? What happened right after?
      What were you feeling?

PART TWO
TRIGGERS

Photo 2

Who is in the photo? How do you know them?

When was the photo taken?

Where were you?

Why were you there?

What was happening when that photo was taken? What happened right after?

What were you feeling?

_____
_____
_____
_____
_____
_____
_____
_____
_____
_____
_____
_____
_____
_____
_____
_____
_____
_____
_____
_____
_____
_____
_____
_____
_____
_____

PART TWO
TRIGGERS

Photo 3

Who is in the photo? How do you know them?

When was the photo taken?

Where were you?

Why were you there?

What was happening when that photo was taken? What happened right after?

What were you feeling?

....
....
....
....
....
....
....
....
....
....
....
....
....
....
....
....
....
....
....
....
....
....
....
....
....

PART TWO
TRIGGERS

Photo 4

Who is in the photo? How do you know them?

When was the photo taken?

Where were you?

Why were you there?

What was happening when that photo was taken? What happened right after?

What were you feeling?

PART TWO
TRIGGERS

Photo 5

Who is in the photo? How do you know them?

When was the photo taken?

Where were you?

Why were you there?

What was happening when that photo was taken? What happened right after?

What were you feeling?

PART TWO
TRIGGERS

Now that you've raided your *own* photo supply, go raid someone else's – someone who has photos with you in them. Think OLD photos with people you can barely remember or not remember at all. Spend some time looking through them and ask the "owner" of the photos questions to fill in the gaps of your memory.

Photo 1

Who is in the photo? How do you know them?

     When was the photo taken?

     Where were you?

     Why were you there?

     What was happening when that photo was taken? What happened right after?

     What were you feeling?

PART TWO
TRIGGERS

Photo 2

Who is in the photo? How do you know them?

    When was the photo taken?

    Where were you?

    Why were you there?

    What was happening when that photo was taken? What happened right after?

    What were you feeling?

PART TWO
TRIGGERS

Photo 3

Who is in the photo? How do you know them?

When was the photo taken?

Where were you?

Why were you there?

What was happening when that photo was taken? What happened right after?

What were you feeling?

PART TWO
TRIGGERS

Photo 4

Who is in the photo? How do you know them?

When was the photo taken?

Where were you?

Why were you there?

What was happening when that photo was taken? What happened right after?

What were you feeling?

PART TWO
TRIGGERS

Photo 5

Who is in the photo? How do you know them?

When was the photo taken?

Where were you?

Why were you there?

What was happening when that photo was taken? What happened right after?

What were you feeling?

PART TWO
TRIGGERS

Finally, since it's been a while since any of us really *printed* a photo, scroll through your various social media platforms and look through images (yours or your friends' or children's) you may have forgotten.

Photo 1

Who is in the photo? How do you know them?

    When was the photo taken?

    Where were you?

    Why were you there?

    What was happening when that photo was taken? What happened right after?

    What were you feeling?

PART TWO
TRIGGERS

Photo 2

Who is in the photo? How do you know them?
- When was the photo taken?
- Where were you?
- Why were you there?
- What was happening when that photo was taken? What happened right after?
- What were you feeling?

PART TWO
TRIGGERS

Photo 3

Who is in the photo? How do you know them?

When was the photo taken?

Where were you?

Why were you there?

What was happening when that photo was taken? What happened right after?

What were you feeling?

PART TWO
TRIGGERS

Photo 4

Who is in the photo? How do you know them?

When was the photo taken?

Where were you?

Why were you there?

What was happening when that photo was taken? What happened right after?

What were you feeling?

PART TWO
TRIGGERS

STORIES WITH FRIENDS

I was recently at a BBQ with three of my five college roommates – a great group of women I only see once a year at best. After a couple beers (and a couple hot dogs) the conversation turned to "Remember when..." and this time it was a story about me; me and my crazy procrastination tactics during college. I had entirely forgotten the insanity that ensued 12 hours before a major paper was due. We laughed and I denied any of it was true, but on the car ride home I made a note of the story in my phone... I'd be able to use that someday when putting together a presentation about NOT procrastinating.

Though years pass and many things change, it never fails that when a couple old friends get together, it doesn't even take a few beers (or a hot dog) for the stories of old to be told (for family, it only takes a holiday dinner table). Sometimes they are old favorites – told and retold 100 times over. Sometimes they're "new" old memories – ones you haven't heard before. Sometimes they sound a lot different than what you remember. For that reason, these "reunions" with friends are perfect opportunities to observe stories in their natural habitat.

Though these "story sessions" may have been the source of some eye-rolling in the past, now that you're committed to finding stories, you'll embrace these story-rich events. If you're up for the challenge, plan a get-together with old friends or family you don't see often, and when the stories start coming out, be capture ready.

Use the following pages to write down stories that were told at a gathering of friends/family.

PART TWO
TRIGGERS

PART TWO
TRIGGERS

PART TWO
TRIGGERS

PART TWO
TRIGGERS

A WALK AROUND THE BLOCK

> *My husband grew up on Coronado Island – a tight-knit community that spans blocks and blocks of homes until reaching the Pacific Ocean. Whenever we're back to visit, we roam the streets and he points out houses as we go, each one with a story: "That's where Josh used to live – we played catch in the street right here until Matt's foot got run over by a car." "That's where our band used to practice." "Here's the alley I ran down after bombing high school graduation with water balloons." It seemed every block had a new story – one he wouldn't have told had we not passed that particular spot on the street. The same was true for my hometown – whenever I bring him, I tell my husband about various random memories that come back to me while traveling familiar streets. Sometimes I surprise myself with a story I had forgotten completely.*

The next time you are in a place you once lived or spent a lot of time, take a nice long walk. Take notice of the landmarks you pass. Though they may not be significant by the city's standards, if they hold a memory of yours, write it down – make a note. Use the following pages as a guide.

Location 1
Where is it?
....
....
....

What happened here?
....
....
....
....

Who would you see here?
....
....
....

How has it changed?
....
....
....
....
....

PART TWO
TRIGGERS

Location 2
Where is it?
....
....
....

What happened here?
....
....
....

Who would you see here?
....
....
....

How has it changed?
....
....
....

Location 3
Where is it?
....
....
....

What happened here?
....
....
....

Who would you see here?
....
....
....

How has it changed?
....
....

Finding Your Story | *Kindra Hall*

PART TWO
TRIGGERS

Location 4

Where is it?
....
....
....

What happened here?
....
....
....

Who would you see here?
....
....
....

How has it changed?
....
....
....

Location 5

Where is it?
....
....
....

What happened here?
....
....
....

Who would you see here?
....
....
....

How has it changed?
....
....
....

PART TWO
TRIGGERS

EXTRA PAGES
If the lines in the individual exercise weren't enough, here is some more space for your stories

PART TWO
TRIGGERS

PART TWO
TRIGGERS

PART TWO
TRIGGERS

PART TWO
TRIGGERS

> *By telling the story it no longer controls me. It's in my venacular, it's the way I see the world.*
>
> – KEVIN KLING

Part Three
THE UGLY STORIES

PART THREE
UGLY STORIES

UGLY STORIES
What They Are

Ahh. The Ugly Stories.

These are the stories we try our best to hide in our closets and shove into the dusty depths of our memories. The ones we want to forget. They are the stories that broke our hearts, that gave us scars, that we regret. Big or small, they are the stories we wished had never happened. Or at the very least, had happened differently. And if we could go back in time, we would… but we can't.

For better or worse, Ugly Stories shape us – they are the ones that alter our course or reveal our true character to others (and reveal it to ourselves if we're willing). And while it's only natural to want to keep them to yourself, Ugly Stories are the most important stories you can tell.

Why It Is Important to Tell Them
In Business

There is a lot of talk right now about authenticity, vulnerability and transparency, particularly in business. The public is calling for (is desperate for) authentic leaders – people who are trustworthy and honest, and that includes not lying by omission. It's not about having nothing to hide; people aren't looking for perfection. They simply want the whole story. Those who are willing to share the moments most people would rather keep to themselves have a distinct advantage over those who aren't so willing.

> *I spent some time working with a CEO whose company focused on getting people out of financial ruin. The CEO himself had, just a few years before starting the company, experienced a financial crisis of his own – divorce, bankruptcy, living in a rundown apartment with no one but his dog for company… you know the story. However, though he was facing" financial ruin," he didn't let it ruin him. He quickly made a turn-around and started a successful, multimillion-dollar company.*
>
> *It was a PERFECT story – an excellent way to say to his audience, "I've been where you are and I can help you get out," and yet, he would not share it. He didn't want to show weakness. Instead, whenever he spoke – to his shareholders, to his clients – he relied on vague rhetoric. His words sounded empty at best, and at worst, left the audience with a subtle sense that he had something to hide. A two-minute story of the struggles he had faced would have solved all of these problems and his business would benefit as a result.*

There is a certain magic to vulnerability. Vulnerability happens when we expose a piece of ourselves that was/is delicate; a topic that is sensitive or uncomfortable, a moment that could be criticized or judged – one that we are ashamed of, or embarrassed of, or sad about. By sharing an Ugly Story and making yourself vulnerable, you are showing your audience that you *trust them*. You trust them enough to be completely open – enough to tell stories others try to hide. Trust by disclosure is reciprocal. By showing them that you trust them with sensitive information, they can be more willing to trust you. It is in that trust that the magic happens.

PART THREE
UGLY STORIES

Telling the Ugly Stories, especially if you are in a leadership role or speaking as an expert, gives your audience an opportunity to relate – to know that you have struggled just as they have struggled or are struggling. Additionally, our Ugly Stories offer unique teaching moments. You can share what you have learned through experience and can spare your audience the pain of learning it the hard way.

Finally, the Ugly Stories are often the most captivating. They are the ones with the most conflict, tension, and drama. We watch a Hero (you) falter and come out on the other side. By telling the stories you wish you could forget, you're actually tapping into the formula that keeps movie theaters full and Hollywood in business.

In Life

Ugly Stories can, in many ways, shackle us; make us feel shameful, sad, and a whole spectrum of other unpleasant (to say the least) emotions. In telling your Ugly Story, you free yourself from it. By making the story public, you conquer it. There is no place for shame to hide when you share the story with the world. So, if for no other reason than personal empowerment, identify the stories that are holding you back and prepare them for telling. And, as an added bonus, the people you choose to share it with will often thank you.

> IT'S A SHALLOW LIFE THAT DOESN'T GIVE A PERSON A FEW SCARS.
> – GARRISON KEILLOR

I was 25 years old and at a storytelling event when a classy woman in her early sixties took the stage and started telling the story of her son when he was a small boy. The story progressed to her son falling in love, having a son of his own, and... in a sudden and tragic turn of events... how he very suddenly fell ill and passed away. The story resolved with a beautiful image of her grandson who had his father's eyes, and in him, the man lived on. Even as a 25-year-old single woman with no children of my own, I felt her pain and grieved her loss. I swallowed hard, struggling to keep my composure, but the teller didn't shed a tear. She had dealt with the tears many years before. Instead, she offered a gift. She shared her saddest moment with an audience of strangers, and in doing so gave us hope – that someday we could be healed enough, strong enough, to tell the story of our most heartbreaking moment.

PART THREE
UGLY STORIES

Finding Your Ugly Stories

If you need help finding your Ugly Stories, below are a series of questions and prompts you can use to uncover them. These are designed to ease you into the process – chances are, there isn't a question I could ask or a prompt I could give you that would unveil your "ugliest" story. Only YOU know what that is. Use these prompts to build your confidence and make you more comfortable about telling the story that *really* needs to be told.

EMBARRASSING MOMENTS

Think of your MOST embarrassing moment.

Where were you?

Who was there?

What happened?

Why were you embarrassed?

Are you STILL embarrassed?

If you could go back, what would you do differently?

PART THREE
UGLY STORIES

Think of another embarrassing moment.
- Where were you?
- Who was there?
- What happened?
- Why were you embarrassed?
- Are you STILL embarrassed?
- If you could go back, what would you do differently?

PART THREE
UGLY STORIES

Think of another embarrassing moment.

    Where were you?

    Who was there?

    What happened?

    Why were you embarrassed?

    Are you STILL embarrassed?

    If you could go back, what would you do differently?

PART THREE
UGLY STORIES

A TIME YOU LIED

Think of a lie you told (start small).

Why did you tell it?

Were you protecting someone (their feelings)?

Were you hiding something?

Were you trying to get out of something?

Was it just for fun?

What happened?

Did the lie work?

Did it backfire?

PART THREE
UGLY STORIES

Think of another lie you told (or time you hid the truth).
- Why did you tell it?
  - Were you protecting someone (their feelings)?
  - Were you hiding something?
  - Were you trying to get out of something?
  - Was it just for fun?
- What happened?
  - Did the lie work?
  - Did it backfire?

PART THREE
UGLY STORIES

THINK OF A TIME YOU CRIED

When there were witnesses.

When you were alone and no one saw.

PART THREE
UGLY STORIES

THINK OF A TIME YOU FAILED...
In a relationship:
A romantic relationship?
A family member?
A friend?

PART THREE
UGLY STORIES

In business:
    As a boss?
    As an employee?
    As a coworker?

PART THREE
UGLY STORIES

Failed yourself:
    Abandoned a goal?
    Underestimated your ability/potential?

PART THREE
UGLY STORIES

THE MEANEST THOUGHT YOU'VE EVER HAD

THE MEANEST THING YOU'VE EVER SAID

PART THREE
UGLY STORIES

SOMETHING THAT STILL MAKES YOU CRINGE WHEN YOU THINK ABOUT IT

IF YOU COULD GO BACK AND CHANGE ONE THING, WHAT WOULD IT BE?

PART THREE
UGLY STORIES

Now it is time to take a risk. Spend some time brainstorming events/emotions/occurrences that *haven't* come up in the previous prompts. Is there something you are particularly private about? Don't worry, writing it down doesn't mean you have to share it. Writing it down *will* however make you more aware of the Ugly Stories you have available to tell.

PART THREE
UGLY STORIES

PART THREE
UGLY STORIES

PART THREE
UGLY STORIES

PART THREE
UGLY STORIES

PART THREE
UGLY STORIES

EXTRA PAGES

If the lines in the individual exercise weren't enough, here is some more space for your stories

PART THREE

UGLY STORIES

PART THREE
UGLY STORIES

PART THREE
UGLY STORIES

PART THREE
UGLY STORIES

PART THREE
UGLY STORIES

PART THREE
UGLY STORIES

PART THREE
UGLY STORIES

Storytelling is by far the most underrated skill in business.
— GARY VAYNERCHUCK

Part Four
TOPIC SPECIFIC STORIES

PART FOUR
TOPIC-SPECIFIC STORIES

TOPIC-SPECIFIC STORIES

Finding topic-specific stories is one of the most challenging aspects of incorporating stories into your presentations. It is a daunting task (like finding a story-needle in a memory-haystack) and the single most common deterrent for even the most hopeful potential-story-users. In my one-on-one work with clients, even as a skilled storyteller myself, this is the part that requires the most work, the most patience, and elicits the most frustration.

> *One day I opened my Facebook account to find a message from an acquaintance in college. This is what it said:*
>
> I am becoming a believer in incorporating stories when speaking to bring the audience in. My question is, How do you think of a story that fits the theme of what you want to say? It feels backward and I've been racking my brain all morning. It seems unnatural to have a theme and then try to recall and retrofit a story. Seems more normal to have something happen that causes you to say, "Hey, I think that is a good analogy.... I'm gonna share it!" Any thoughts?
>
> *Yes, I had some thoughts – several thoughts actually. Here they are in no particular order:*
> *~ Yes. It can feel backward.*
> *~ Hurray for becoming a "believer"!*
> *~ Yes. You're likely to be racking your brain all morning.*
> *~ Yes. It's great when something happens and you can say, "Hey, that's a great analogy, I'll use it!" but unfortunately that doesn't often happen – or at least not at the exact moment we need it to.*
> *~ I can't believe how small (and awesome) the world has become; that a girl I kind-of-knew in college is now contacting me, nearly a decade later, to ask about storytelling.*

While I am a strong believer that *anytime* you go in search of a story you will find great (though sometimes unrelated) material, I understand that sometimes there isn't *time* for an extended story journey. Often we're in a pinch – we need a story and we need it fast.

Here's the good news. If you have worked your way through this program and have completed the exercises, it is likely you have already uncovered the *memories* you need to tell the *story* you need to illustrate your point. If you *haven't* worked your way through this notebook but rather thumbed through to this page, I can still help you.

Below is a list of common topics or themes people are asked to speak on. Find your topic, or one that is closely related, and follow the guide below. It will lead you to the prompts that are most likely to house relevant material. If you haven't already, **complete the prompt in the suggested section FIRST,** then follow the remaining instructions

PART FOUR
TOPIC-SPECIFIC STORIES

LEADERSHIP
Look for stories in:

Your first job (Common Experiences)
Did you witness any acts of leadership from others?
Did you show any leadership?

Least favorite boss (Common Experiences)
There could be stories here of "leadership gone wrong."

Sports you played (Lists, Phase 1)
Sports experiences are rich in leadership.
Did you lead your team to victory? Or did someone else?
Was there a coach who was a great leader? Or a bad one?

Jobs you had (Lists, Phase 1)
In the various jobs you've had, did you ever have a leadership role? What was it? What did you do well in that role? What would you have done differently? (Think of specific occurrences.)

Bosses (Lists, Phase 1)
Did you learn anything about leadership (for better or worse) from any of your former (or current) bosses?

Coworkers (Lists, Phase 1
Did you learn anything about leadership (for better or worse) from any of your former (or current) coworkers?

Scariest thing to happen to you (Lists, Phase 3)
In your scariest moment, were you a leader?
What could you learn about leadership from that experience?

Proudest moment (Lists, Phase 3)
In your proudest moment, were you a leader?
Would others be proud of your leadership? Who?

A time when you failed (in business) (Part 3)
Was it due to a lack of leadership?
Did you learn anything from that experience?
What would you do differently in terms of leadership?

Use the following pages to answer questions for this section.

PART FOUR
TOPIC-SPECIFIC STORIES

PART FOUR

TOPIC-SPECIFIC STORIES

PART FOUR
TOPIC-SPECIFIC STORIES

PART FOUR

TOPIC-SPECIFIC STORIES

PART FOUR
TOPIC-SPECIFIC STORIES

SALES

Let's do a little variation of the previous exercise. While you CAN, go back and look through some of the exercises you have already completed. Here are a few "Sales-Specific" prompts that can help you find stories on this topic.

Your first sale
- What were you selling?
- How much did it cost?
- How old were you?
- Who was your buyer?
- What was their story?
- How did it make you feel?
- What did you do wrong (and even though you did it wrong you still made the sale)?
- What did you do with the money you earned?

Your most meaningful sale – the one you remember the most
- What were you selling?
- When was it?
- How much did it cost?
- Who was your buyer?
- What was their story?
- Why does it stand out?
- Was it a challenging sale?

The sale that got away
- What were you selling?
- When was it?
- How much did it cost?
- Who was your buyer?
- What was their story?
- What went wrong?
- What did you do to try to save the sale?
- What could you have done differently?

The time YOU bought something partially because of the skill of the person selling it
- What were you buying?
- Why?
- When was it?
- How much did it cost?
- What do you remember about the salesperson?
- What did they say/do to convince you?

PART FOUR
TOPIC-SPECIFIC STORIES

Your most satisfied customers

Think about five people who have purchased your product and have had success with it.

Take a few lines to write about each one.

      What was their story before your product?

      How did you meet them?

      What has changed in their life since making the purchase?

Use the following pages to answer those questions.

PART FOUR
TOPIC-SPECIFIC STORIES

PART FOUR
TOPIC-SPECIFIC STORIES

PART FOUR

TOPIC-SPECIFIC STORIES

PART FOUR
TOPIC-SPECIFIC STORIES

PART FOUR
TOPIC-SPECIFIC STORIES

MOTIVATION, CHANGE MANAGEMENT, PERSONAL GROWTH, OVERCOMING OBSTACLES, SUCCESS & ACHIEVEMENT

If you are speaking on any of these topics, take a look at what you wrote in these earlier prompts and then answer the following questions:

From Chapter 3: Common Experiences

Your first kiss

Were there obstacles involved in this event?

How did you overcome them?

Did you experience growth from this experience/rite of passage?

Your favorite teachers

What did they do to motivate you?

Did they challenge you?

Did they encourage growth in you?

From Chapter 4: Turning Points

Birth of a child

What growth did you personally experience during this event?

What were some obstacles you faced?

How did you manage the many changes that come with this experience?

The day you decided (or were told) you were getting divorced

What growth did you personally experience during this event?

What were some obstacles you faced?

How did you manage the many changes that came with this experience?

The death of a loved one

What growth did you personally experience during this event?

What were some obstacles you faced?

How did you manage the many changes that came with this experience?

From Chapters 5 & 6: Lists and Triggers

Look at each of the items on the lists in this chapter and ask if any of the people/events:

    Led to a moment of growth

    Involved obstacles you had to overcome

    Acted as a catalyst for significant change in you/for you

    Were particularly inspiring to you

Particularly in Phases 3 and 4 – Those prompts elicit a little more depth and are perfect for stories on these topics.

PART FOUR
TOPIC-SPECIFIC STORIES

From Part 3: The Ugly Stories

Perhaps the strongest stories for Personal Growth, Change Management, Success & Achievement... all of these... are waiting in the Ugly Story section of this book. Go back through, look at the stories you've already recorded (or complete the exercises now) and then ask yourself these additional questions:

Did this person/event:

Lead to a moment of growth

Involve obstacles you had to overcome

Act as a catalyst for significant change in you/for you

Make you feel inspired

Use the following pages to answer those questions.

PART FOUR
TOPIC-SPECIFIC STORIES

PART FOUR
TOPIC-SPECIFIC STORIES

PART FOUR
TOPIC-SPECIFIC STORIES

PART FOUR
TOPIC-SPECIFIC STORIES

PART FOUR
TOPIC-SPECIFIC STORIES

COMMUNICATION SKILLS, TEAM BUILDING:

Relationship (both personal and professional) stories are great for illustrating points about the importance of communication and team building. Take a look back at these Prompts:

From Chapter 5: Lists, Phase 1

Coworkers & Bosses: Look at each of the names on these lists.

> Who did you work well with? Why?
>
> Were you responsible for completing projects together? Was that easy? Difficult? Why?
>
> Was there ever a time you felt misunderstood by a coworker or boss? What happened?
>> How did it get resolved?
>
> Did any of these people teach you something about communication?
>
> Did any of these people teach you something about working on a team?

From Chapter 5: Lists, Phase 3

Your biggest fights

> Where did the communication break down?
>
> What could have been done differently?
>
> What did you learn from the experience?

From Chapter 6: Triggers

Stories with Friends

By nature, since these stories come from conversations with others, you are able to get someone else's take on an event. This outside perspective can shed light on how communication worked or fell apart.

Use the following pages to answer those questions.

PART FOUR
TOPIC-SPECIFIC STORIES

PART FOUR
TOPIC-SPECIFIC STORIES

PART FOUR
TOPIC-SPECIFIC STORIES

PART FOUR

TOPIC-SPECIFIC STORIES

PART FOUR
TOPIC-SPECIFIC STORIES

As I said at the beginning of this section, finding Topic-Specific stories is definitely challenging. For this reason it is critical that you not only develop the skill for *recalling* stories that have already happened, but you must also work at being able to spot a story as it's happening. That is what I will teach you next.

In case you're interested, here is the email I sent back to my friend:

Hi [shall remain nameless]! This is a great question and I'm so glad you're bringing stories into your presentations. It is tough when you have a set theme and have to think of a story to fit the THEME instead of choosing a theme based on a story you want to TELL, but the reality is, that's often the case, especially in business.

So, there are a couple of things you can do. First, start with the purpose of the presentation. What is the goal? What do you want people to walk away feeling or what do you want them motivated to DO? Make sure that is clear – it will help you choose the RIGHT story for that audience/purpose.

Second, start digging around in the areas of your life where the most stories are hiding or where you have learned the most lessons. If the message you're trying to convey is about Leadership or Perseverance, go straight to your memories from playing sports [she was a collegiate athlete] – great stories hide there. If it's about Compromise or Interpersonal Relationships, I find husbands and marriage great sources of material. Finally, think about the various roles you've played in your life – daughter, athlete, friend, student, professional, etc. – and what some of your best (or worst) memories are in each one of those roles; those will lead you to great stories.

I know it's not a quick fix, but that is one way you can start brainstorming ideas and finding stories. AND, every time you DO think of a story, even if it's not related to THIS particular speech, make a note of it because you might be able to use it for another project. There's obviously a lot more to it, but that's a place to start.

PART FOUR
TOPIC-SPECIFIC STORIES

EXTRA PAGES
If the lines in the individual exercise weren't enough, here is some more space for your stories

PART FOUR
TOPIC-SPECIFIC STORIES

PART FOUR
TOPIC-SPECIFIC STORIES

PART FOUR
TOPIC-SPECIFIC STORIES

PART FOUR
TOPIC-SPECIFIC STORIES

PART FOUR
TOPIC-SPECIFIC STORIES

> *Storytelling is not what I do for a living – it is how I do all that I do while I am living.* -DONALD DAVIS

Part Five

STORIES THAT ARE HAPPENING NOW

PART FIVE

STORIES THAT ARE HAPPENING NOW

STORIES THAT ARE HAPPENING NOW

Becoming a skilled user of story requires that you not only are able to access stories that have happened to you in the past, but that you can recognize a story as it is happening *now* (or at least, as it happened earlier today). This can be challenging, partly because recognizing a story as it happens requires us to really engage in the world around us (and disengage from technology).

Putting the cellphone down is an unofficial first step to this process. Don't worry. I'm not going to step up on a soapbox – I am as guilty as anyone. If there is even a 15-second lull in conversation/checkout line/traffic, I am scrolling to find *anything* of interest. Quite frankly, purchasing my iPhone has led to a noticeable decrease in new material. I miss out on the scraps of story that are happening around me – and you will, too.

That being said, if you have completed the earlier exercises in this workbook you are ready to learn this next, extremely important skill. You've built up your story muscle and are ready for the heavy lifting of recognizing a story the moment it happens.

The following is a series of exercises, prompts and strategies you can use to find stories that are happening now.

AT END OF THE DAY

As the day comes to a close, you put the kids to bed, you settle in on the couch, you're about to watch whatever your DVR captured (or maybe you're in bed about to turn out the light and finally sleep); take a quick moment to answer these questions:

Location 1: ....

    What were you doing there?

....
....
....
....

    Who did you talk to?
    (including people who helped you: cashiers, servers, receptionists, etc)

....
....
....
....
....

PART FIVE
STORIES THAT ARE HAPPENING NOW

Who did you see?
(including people who simply caught your eye: a dad with a small child)

....
....
....
....

Was there anything that made you feel:
- ☐ Happy ☐ Nervous ☐ Excited ☐ Annoyed ☐ ....
- ☐ Frustrated ☐ Jealous ☐ Loved ☐ Proud ☐ ....
- ☐ Satisfied ☐ Angry ☐ Uneasy ☐ Beautiful ☐ ....

Why? or How?

....
....
....
....
....
....
....

Did anything make you say AHA?
Did anything make you say UGH?
Did anything make you say, "Hmm. That was interesting"?

....
....
....
....
....
....
....
....

PART FIVE
STORIES THAT ARE HAPPENING NOW

Location 2: ....

What were you doing there?

....
....

Who did you talk to?
(including people who helped you: cashiers, servers, receptionists, etc)

....
....
....
....

Who did you see?
(including people who simply caught your eye: a dad with a small child)

....
....
....
....

Was there anything that made you feel:
☐ Happy   ☐ Nervous   ☐ Excited   ☐ Annoyed   ☐ ....
☐ Frustrated ☐ Jealous   ☐ Loved   ☐ Proud   ☐ ....
☐ Satisfied ☐ Angry   ☐ Uneasy   ☐ Beautiful ☐ ....

Why? or How?

....
....
....
....
....
....
....
....
....

PART FIVE
STORIES THAT ARE HAPPENING NOW

Did anything make you say AHA?

Did anything make you say UGH?

Did anything make you say, "Hmm. That was interesting"?

PART FIVE
STORIES THAT ARE HAPPENING NOW

OTHER PROMPTS
Here are a few additional questions you can ask yourself at the end of the day that might produce a story.

    Did anything happen that usually doesn't?

    Did you do something you don't normally do?

        Why?

        How did that turn out?

    Did you do something you DO usually do but the outcome was somehow different?

        How was it different?

        Was it a good thing?

    When you answered the question, "How was your day?"... what did you say?

        Why?

PART FIVE
STORIES THAT ARE HAPPENING NOW

IN THE MOMENT

Identifying a story the moment it happens can sometimes be easy – if it's a big moment (car accident) or an out of the ordinary experience (bungee jumping). But, for the most part, the subtle stories that occur as a result of normal life can be more difficult to spot while they're happening. It requires a shift in our behavior and a degree of emotional self-awareness/reflection that isn't otherwise required for everyday living.

Here are a few strategies to help you heighten your awareness, and therefore effectiveness, when it comes to spotting these "everyday" stories:

> At any given time, did you sense a distinct shift in your emotion?
>> Did you shift from positive to negative? Negative to positive?
>> What happened to create that shift?

....
....
....
....
....
....
....
....
....
....

> Did you develop an opinion about someone/something?
>> In these moments, what was your internal dialogue?
>> What does that say about you?

....
....
....
....
....
....
....
....
....
....

PART FIVE
STORIES THAT ARE HAPPENING NOW

As a rule, take note of how you feel. Your emotions will lead you to your stories:

- A shiver down your spine
- A subtle feeling of discomfort
- Any pain
- Any excitement or anticipation

In preparation for this chapter, I challenged myself to identify a story as it happened today. I was nervous I might prove myself wrong... that stories AREN'T always happening. Fortunately for me (and everything I believe in) a mere three hours into my morning a story appeared.

I was walking around a local antique shop looking for an old-fashioned iron for the upcoming photo shoot for the cover of my book Otherwise Untold. As I wandered among the rooms of treasures, I passed a woman who was clearly an antique shopping fanatic. I overheard her telling a store clerk about her great-grandmother's china, watched her contemplate purchasing a large wooden chicken, and finally, as I was about to leave the store (iron-less) I heard her telling another shopper about her daughter. It was this interaction that caught my attention.

Apparently her daughter had, at one point, started collecting "milk glass" pieces (whatever that is). This had thrilled the woman and as I headed toward the door I heard her say with a joy in her voice "It was so fun to come into places like this and buy a piece for her...." Then her voice trailed off, she took a breath and continued, "But... she just told me the other day, after only two years, she's stopped collecting milk glass... that I shouldn't buy here anymore... that she had too much." I turned to see the woman shake her head – she was more than disappointed, she was genuinely sad that she could no longer buy milk glass for her daughter.

No. It was more than that.

PART FIVE
STORIES THAT ARE HAPPENING NOW

She was disappointed she could no longer participate in her daughter's life – at the very least, in that way.

As I walked out to my car I thought of that woman's daughter.
What a B-word!
Was it SO HARD for her to keep collecting "milk glass"?
Was it SO HARD for her to pack the "milk glass" in a plastic bin in the garage?
Didn't she know that by telling her mom to "stop buying milk glass" she was actually breaking her heart? Clearly her (slightly odd) mother loved having a way to connect with her daughter – loved having a way to bring her daughter joy in a way that she herself was passionate about.
What kind of daughter would treat her mother that way? If only the daughter could have heard the heartbreak in her well-meaning-mother's voice that day in the antique store....

And then, just five footsteps out the door, I heard the whispers of conversations I had had with my own mother:
"Mom! Stop! I know YOU love pottery, but it's not my thing. We have no use for it. It clutters my cupboards. Please! Stop buying me pottery."
"Mom! Stop buying me nativity scenes! I know YOU love nativity scenes, but it's not my thing. We have no use for them. They clutter my house at Christmas. Please! Stop buying me nativity scenes!"

...

In that one moment I learned two important things.
One. It was unfair for me to pass such harsh judgment on someone I didn't know. Often when we do so, the person turns out to be not-so-different from ourselves.

Two. I needed to have more sensitivity toward my mother. She could very well be having the same conversation with a stranger in a pottery store – with the same sound of heartbreak in her voice. I would hate for that to be the case. And to change it meant I needed to change.

This "story" happened in a moment. It wasn't by any means profound or extraordinary; I was, quite frankly, eavesdropping on a conversation that was none of my business. However, by identifying my emotions (the "What a B-word" emotion) and taking a moment to reflect on said emotion, a story revealed itself and, more important, I learned an important lesson.

I should note that the science of adding details and developing the plot/resolve are techniques that I will cover in **Crafting Your Story**. But none of the crafting matters if you don't have the raw material. Start today – look for the stories that are happening all around you.

PART FIVE

STORIES THAT ARE HAPPENING NOW

EXTRA PAGES

If the lines in the individual exercise weren't enough, here is some more space for your stories

PART FIVE
STORIES THAT ARE HAPPENING NOW

PART FIVE

STORIES THAT ARE HAPPENING NOW

PART FIVE
STORIES THAT ARE HAPPENING NOW

PART FIVE
STORIES THAT ARE HAPPENING NOW

PART FIVE
STORIES THAT ARE HAPPENING NOW

> *Great stories happen to those who can tell them.* —IRA GLASS

Part Six
ADDITIONAL THINGS

PART SIX
ADDITIONAL THINGS

ADDITIONAL THINGS

BE CAPTURE-READY.

Once you open the door to recalling stories, the stories will keep coming through. Sometimes they will be fragments of memories (the name of an old neighborhood friend, a weekend trip you took with your college buddies), sometimes they will be entire stories already ready for telling. This is a wonderful side effect of actively finding your stories – your conscious effort has *subconscious* ramifications. Wonderful if and only if you have a way to capture the stories that come to you; otherwise the side effect is totally frustrating, because you realize the great material that's slipping through your fingers... because often, as quickly as they come, they slip away again.

I recommend carrying a small, spiral-bound notebook and pen in your purse or pocket wherever you go. When a story or story fragment resurfaces, make a note. It doesn't need to be complete – it just needs to be enough so that you know what it means when you read it later.

> *I've moved many, many, many times and every time I do, I go through the process of throwing away the stuff I don't need. I'm pretty ruthless - I throw away objects, clothing, décor, gifts, etc., knowing I'll forget them before I have time to regret them. However, the one thing that ALWAYS survives are my notebooks. I have stacks of notebooks from all phases of my life that contain scraps of memories (scraps of stories) that would otherwise be lost completely. To me, these notebooks contain more value than any other item I own. They are simply irreplaceable.*

If a notebook is too much (or if you'll buy one and never remember to carry it with you), then use your phone – either a notepad app or voice recorder function. While I *prefer* seeing the curves of my own handwriting, I too have used my phone (I text message myself way more than the average person) to capture otherwise forgotten memories. Just be sure to back it up.

DON'T JUDGE.

I've said it before.
I'll say it again and again.
It's easy to *not* write something down because it's "too small," or "I would never use this" or you "don't know where it would fit." It's easy to write off a memory as irrelevant or a detail as insignificant. However, before you start judging your stories before they've hatched, consider this:

The small memories add color to the big ones. This is a concept we will discuss more in future trainings, but for the time being think about the speakers who have impacted you the most; there is a deliberate, subtle, seemingly casual depth. It exists in the effortless thoroughness of the stories they share. This depth separates the greats from the rest and can only be achieved when the speaker has an awareness of the smaller details. Judging the outwardly insignificant pieces of your story inhibits your ability to connect with your audience in

PART SIX
ADDITIONAL THINGS

that subtle, skillful way. Often, in the midst of the small, pointless stories, emerges a big one. Give it time – give it space to happen.

TALK "*ABOUT*" THE TIME... TELL "*ABOUT*" THE STORY.

It is easy to get tripped up when you try to "tell" the story. There's a natural desire to tell it right the very first time. The pressure of that mindset can quickly halt the creative process – or any process, really. Instead of focusing on telling the story proper, focus first on telling *about* the story. Tell *about* the time your car broke down in dangerous circumstances and how you relied on the kindness of strangers to get you and your family home safely. Tell *about* the time you were in eighth grade and embarrassed in front of the girl you liked. Tell *about* the crazy antics of you and your best friend in college. The "about" gives you room to remember and space to enjoy. From there the "right" version of the story will emerge.

> *Many of my client meetings involve a lot of apologies during that first appointment – the client apologizes before every memory – apologizing for not "telling it right." They'll preface every new thought/story with "I don't know if this helps" or "This might be stupid but...." I always assure them that no story is going to be perfect the first time you say it, but no story will ever happen if you don't say it that first time.*

DISCIPLINE.

Storytelling is a skill, and just like any skill, it takes discipline to develop. We've all been on the receiving end of a poorly told story – one that gets lost on tangents, focuses on irrelevant details, and lasts many minutes beyond what was necessary. It's true that storytelling comes very natural to us humans, but *good* storytelling, *effective* storytelling, requires *more*. And it begins with a breadth of material to choose from. Be disciplined in searching for, finding, and recording your stories. This discipline is the main delineation between the greats and the rest.

> *I once sat beside Donald Davis - the greatest storyteller I have ever known - right before he was to take the stage at a storytelling festival in Arizona. I had heard Donald tell LIVE many times before, had been listening to his audio recordings since I was a child, and was pretty sure there wasn't a story he told that I didn't already know. Sitting there beside him as the emcee recited the litany of awards and honors Donald has received, I watched as he pulled from his pocket a well-loved 8 ½ by 11 ½ sheet of paper. From over his shoulder I caught a glimpse of what appeared to be nonsense - chicken scratching I couldn't really identify cluttered the page. He looked at it for a moment, as if to refresh his memory, refolded it, and placed it carefully in his pocket as he rose from his chair to uproarious applause and approached the stage. I spent the next hour listening to a story I had never heard before. And it became clear.*

PART SIX
ADDITIONAL THINGS

On that single piece of paper was a lifetime of memories/cues for stories to tell. Sure, there were favorites – stories that people would request time and again… but Donald was certainly no one-hit-wonder. During a career that had spanned several decades, Donald remains disciplined in finding more stories, recording more memories, and essentially expanding a repertoire that means he can be hired over and over for decades to come.

WHAT DID I LEARN.

This is the last "Additional Things to Consider" I want you to consider. After every experience you recall, every memory that comes back to you, take a moment and ask yourself, "What did I learn?" or "Who did I become as a result of that experience?" Even small things can change us – and it is that change that makes for the most interesting stories. Taking the time to ask yourself that question will, in and of itself, make you a more effective storyteller. It will help you determine which stories to tell for what audiences, and ensure that your message is targeted and resonant.

This single question also marks the starting line for **Crafting Your Story**.

Conclusion

YOU FOUND IT!

That's it.

You wanted to become a better storyteller. You wanted to incorporate stories into your business life or your personal life. You wanted to connect with your audience. You wanted your message to persuade, to motivate or simply to resonate.

But you wondered if you even had a story to tell....

Well wonder no more because now you do.
Not just one... but pages of them.
You have everything you need to connect, persuade, motivate, and resonate. All of it.

Never again will you be left wondering where or how to start. Never again will you think you do not have a story to tell. You do. And you know exactly where to go to find them.

Your stories are scrawled upon the pages of this book. Some of them are big – your proudest moments or your most painful. Some of the stories are small, just scraps of memories – people you once knew, places you once visited, dreams you once had. Some of them are simple... everyday stories that happen to everyday people. Remember, these are the stories that are relevant, familiar, and therefore effective when communicating with the masses.

As you turn the final pages of this workbook I want you to remember that becoming a skilled storyteller doesn't end here. Stories will come to you and happen to you at any given moment. Be ready to capture them, and most important, remember what I've taught you throughout this entire process – don't judge! Indeed, not *everything* is a story... but anything *could* be. Continue to watch for them, listen for them, and let stories come to you.

Regardless of the size or scope, this book is now filled with stories – YOUR stories.
All that is left to do is tell them.
And when you do, know that I will be the first to stand up and applaud.

About the Author

Kindra Hall has over 20 years of storytelling experience in performance and coaching. She has received national accolades for her skill and has presented for audiences as large as 15,000. Kindra served on the Board of Directors for the National Storytelling Network and completed her master's thesis on the role of story in organizational socialization. Kindra has also told at the most prestigious festival in the world: the National Storytelling Festival in Jonesborough, Tennessee. Kindra is widely recognized for her wisdom and wit in her storytelling approach. She is also the author of the book Otherwise Untold: A Collection of Stories Most People Would Keep to Themselves.

Kindra is married and lives in Phoenix with her husband, son and daughter.

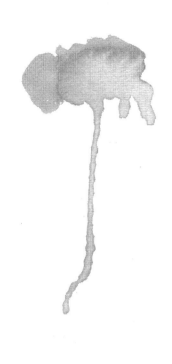